GIN
DISTILLED

GIN

DISTILLED

THE ESSENTIAL GUIDE
FOR GIN LOVERS

EBURY
PRESS

10 9 8 7 6 5 4 3 2 1

Ebury Press, an imprint of Ebury F
20 Vauxhall Bridge Road,
London SW1V 2SA

Ebury Press is part of the Penguin Random House group of companies
whose addresses can be found at global.penguinrandomhouse.com

Penguin
Random House
UK

Copyright © Gin Foundry 2018

Olivier Ward has asserted his right to be identified as the author of this
Work in accordance with the Copyright, Designs and Patents Act 1988

First published by Ebury Press in 2018

www.penguin.co.uk

A CIP catalogue record for this book is available from the British Library

ISBN 9781529102857

Design by seagulls.net
Illustrations by Angeline Balayn
Typeset in 11/14 pt GillSansNova-Book by Jouve (UK), Milton Keynes
Printed and bound in Great Britain by Clays Ltd, Elcograf S.p.A.

MIX
Paper from
responsible sources
FSC
www.fsc.org
FSC® C018179

Penguin Random House is committed to a
sustainable future for our business, our readers
and our planet. This book is made from Forest
Stewardship Council® certified paper.

CONTENTS

INTRODUCTION

There has never been a better time to enjoy gin in our opinion. Call it the 'Ginaissance', or the 'Gin'trification' of society (mainly to get the puns out the way and not return to them again) because gin has never experienced the highs it is soaring towards today.

The aim of this book is simple: to distil the world of contemporary gin into an accessible 'overnight' guide. While the variety of gin on offer today is exciting, with more choice can come greater uncertainty – what gin would you like in your G&T or Martini when you are faced with a menu of 30 options? How should it be served when more than one mixer or garnish is on offer? Is there a best way to drink different gins? This book hopes to act as a one-stop shop to demystify this glorious spirit and enable you to explore, experiment and enjoy gin with confidence.

There are so many varied and complex flavour profiles that push the category out from the classic juniper forward offerings of yesteryear. There has been a rejuvenation of old styles of gin, alongside the invention of new ones from all over the world, all of which cater to the tastes of the modern drinker. We'll run through the different styles of gins available, the brands that showcase each style to its fullest, and how best to serve each one.

You'll find the modern history of gin here, as we put our focus on the rise of craft gin as we know it today. The history of gin stretches back to the sixteenth century, and there are many excellent books already written on its distant (and sometimes depraved) past. So here we have decided to look at the not-so-well-known story of gin from the 1950s onwards — from gin's fall from favour, to its resurrection by the big conglomerates, which eventually paved the way for the craft gin movement that has changed and reinvigorated the way we enjoy gin.

The explosion of botanical profiles means that the drinking and buying of gin can be approached in the same way as a fine wine. Moreover, understanding the different ways gin can be made is essential for knowing what you're drinking and defining what you like. We will cover how gin is made, discuss how to taste gin, what to look for when ordering or buying gin, and what to place a value on.

While we celebrate sipping gins here and the complex botanicals that define them, we don't put gin on a pedestal. Nothing is sacred when it comes to serving gin and home infusions are simply too good not to be included in this book. Finally, no guide to gin would be complete without some advice on how best to mix it and we've included the finest cocktail recipes here too.

We hope you enjoy the read, and we'll see you at the bar.

Gin Foundry

A PERFECT STORM: THE MODERN HISTORY OF GIN

The story of modern gin starts with its demise.

After its last hurrah in the fifties, what followed were decades of neglect and falling fortunes. The swinging sixties ushered in flower power, men on the moon, microwave dinners and pre-mixed cocktails. Gin, along with the bartender's craft of classic cocktail making, declined in favour of convenience experiences. When it came to booze trends, this didn't just mean vodka began its ascent, it meant gin's almost complete eradication . . .

Despite tense relations with Russia during the Cold War era, by the time of the tumble of the Berlin Wall and the Hoff prancing about in a piano keyboard scarf, even the holy grail of gin cocktails, the Martini, had become more commonly served as a Vodka Martini and made using a Russian spirit.

Fortunately, one gin prevailed in these dark times: Bombay Dry Gin. Launched in 1960, 'Bombay Dry' was the brainchild of entrepreneur Allan Subin. Having previously worked in the drinks industry at Seagram's, the Madison Avenue based ad man had spotted the opportunity for a new gin brand. Inspired by some of the original gins of the late eighteenth century and, in particular, that of the pioneer Thomas Dakin (whose distillery is now known as G&J Distillers), he decided to create a gin that embodied the elegance of the 1920s and which had strong connections to English history – both elements he knew would appeal to an American market.

Within five years, Bombay Dry Gin was achieving sales of over 100,000 bottles per year, which even by today's standards was an impressive start. This steady growth continued throughout the seventies (even forcing new stills to be commissioned to keep up production), despite it supposedly being a period in which gin was out of fashion.

Bombay Dry Gin was, unfortunately, the exception to the rule and the seventies were, for the most part, a flat line for most gin makers. Simply put, gin wasn't cool and hadn't been for years. By the eighties, the big drinks companies were almost entirely focused on the success of their flagship vodkas.

Thankfully, in a moment of daring brilliance, Bombay Sapphire was launched in 1988. With an updated recipe formula that built on the success of Bombay Dry, and packaged in what has since become an iconic blue bottle, it may not have been an instant success story, but it is clear that the brand captured the attention of a new generation. Years later, this is now widely credited as a turning point that marked the dawn of a new era.

THE FOUNDATIONS FOR A COMEBACK

The nineties were where much of the craft gin movement built its foundations. While it would be nice to be able to say that Bombay set a trend to premium-ise, it was such a novel concept that it was an outlier and it took years for marketeers to understand why it was successful and look to emulate it (something that can be seen in the noughties, more on this later). For the multinationals, gin's comeback actually began with some shrewd economics in order to compete against the popularity of vodka. Gordon's, Greenall's and Plymouth lowered their ABV to 37.5% and thus reduced the cost per bottle to make it a more affordable choice for consumers. Combined with a notable re-investment in marketing efforts, gin was moving back to the mainstream (albeit in a watered-down form and aimed at the cheap end of the market).

The next seismic shift for the larger brand names occurred in 1997, with the merger of the two biggest drinks companies: Guinness and Grand Metropolitan, which included United Distillers and I.D.V, forming the behemoth Diageo.

Not only did the move force competition authorities to cut it down to size (Bombay Original and Sapphire was sold to Bacardi, for example), it triggered a quick scramble to consolidate brand propositions in other companies, so that they would be able to square up to Diageo. While it sounds particularly unromantic to say that hard economics and the establishment sharpening its elbows should take any credit, it was predominantly these two factors that laid the ground work for gin's comeback.

The mass investment into the gin category that these factors created was a vital first step in the story of gin as we know it today. Bombay may have been the first to show that 'premium-ising' would be the way to succeed in the new era, but it is clear to see that gin needed a dose of hard economics to find a mass audience, before an injection of cool could even stand a chance of gaining traction.

By the year 2000, the fruits of both movements' labour had sown the seeds for what was about to come for the multinationals, and one by one they all released premium versions of their flagship spirits. Diageo added Tanqueray No. Ten (2000) and eclipsed expectations to such an extent that Gordon's Distiller's Cut (released in 2004) is largely forgotten. William Grant & Sons launched Hendrick's (2001) and Pernod Ricard added Beefeater 24 (2007), having already restored Plymouth to its original strength and relaunched in 1998.

Such major companies making that kind of investment and those kinds of launches would have made an impact to change the perception of gin no matter what the state of the market. However, once the independently owned smaller brands and the craft distilling movement that had been bubbling up in hot spots across the world added their offerings into the mix, it would change the picture entirely.

THE BIRTH OF CRAFT

In 1994, in a quiet corner of France at the heart of the Cognac industry, a tenacious distiller named Alexandre Gabriel finally, after much persistence, received approval to distil gin in the 'off' season of the region's annual Cognac production.

By French AOC laws, producers could only distil Cognac from November through March and, after that, the region's beautiful pot stills lay idle. Knowing that, as a spirit redistilled on a neutral alcohol base, gin is not confined to seasonal production and can be made at any time, Gabriel had been seeking permission to make it for years, systematically facing a barrage of French bureaucracy.

In 1995, using the recipe for gin that Gabriel had first developed in 1989, Citadelle Gin was born. On the nose, there's a prominent juniper note to Citadelle Gin, adding depth and a forest-like backdrop to candied orange peel. Inhale deeply and you'll detect the exotic whiff of cardamom in the mix too. To taste, juniper and citrus are again apparent upfront with a dry, satisfyingly peppery finish. It's a classic gin by modern standards and one that we love returning to time and again, especially with a generous orange peel as a garnish in a G&T.

Given the global gin revival was in its infancy though, Citadelle Gin was more than a decade ahead of its time. However, Gabriel's use of a small pot still and time-honoured traditional methods, well ahead of the first examples of similar distilleries in the US and then the UK, meant it was the first of what many would consider a 'craft gin' and marks him as one of the earliest pioneers.

As we've mentioned, for the larger players, gin's global revival really started to gain momentum from 2000 onwards. In the UK, their bottles were on the shelves alongside gins like Martin Miller's Gin and Broker's Gin, which were created and launched in the late nineties. Whitley Neill, Blackwoods, London No.1 and Hayman's quickly joined in the early noughties and, with one building on the success of the other, they helped to showcase the ever increasing range of options available. These independents, running in parallel to the major names, were starting to have an impact and become contenders themselves. In doing so, they paved the way for even more new names to emerge.

With legislation preventing distillation on stills less than 500 litres (132 US gallons) in Britain, either larger 'third party' contractors with years of experience or existing distilleries were the ones doing the production of most of these new independent gins. This meant that they had no real volume restrictions and could be made in large enough quantities to be affordably priced domestically, as well as fulfil demands for export around the world. So despite operating on minute budgets in comparison to the multinationals, these independents were operating at sufficient volume and with enough savvy to be able to thrive – something that many didn't think would happen.

The 'craft' scene we know now would not exist were it not for these years of the larger companies developing the market and the pioneering independents adding to it by showing there was diversity in the category. There would be no Tarquin's Gin without Sipsmith and no Sipsmith without Hendrick's. Equally, there would be no Hendrick's without Bombay Sapphire and there would be no Bombay without Gordon's. The story of craft distilling and modern gin is that of one company building on the success of its predecessor and contributing to propel the category forward, not of a sudden brand leader disrupting the market alone.

Independents are all good and well, but what ultimately made the biggest impact was the shift from often third party-made contract distilled gins made on behalf of a brand owner to numerous micro-producers joining the fray and making their own. We've spoken about Citadelle, but the greatest number of small operations launching gins was in the USA and the country can confidently lay the biggest claim to the origins of the 'craft revolution'.

In 2000, there were around 60 small distilleries across the USA: Junípero and Leopold Bros being two notable trailblazing gin brands. In less than a decade, there were well over 200 others. Many of the early British craft distillers, including Sipsmith and Chase, found their inspiration from trips to the USA during this time.

There are numerous underlying reasons why the US was so quick to embrace craft distilling, but there are two central factors to consider: a strong hobby-brewing scene keen on the idea of making their own, and so many variables in local state liquor laws that had a net effect of reducing national competition and (unintentionally) allowing more local distilleries to thrive. By 2010, craft distilling had a foothold across the US, and its influence created ripples that sent a wave across the world.

THE RETURN OF THE COCKTAIL

With a rise in gin production in both the UK and in the US, there were two other factors that came into play during the noughties to boost the category's profile. The first was a general growth in interest amongst those with disposable income in knowing where their food and drink came from, and wanting to shop local and favour 'small batch and artisan'. The second, and most crucial, was the start of the craft cocktail movement.

As a spirit that depends on the clever balancing of the botanical flavours that define it, as well as the individual flavours combining to become more than the sum of their parts, gin greatly benefitted from a movement that encouraged a passion for flavour and craftsmanship. Buzzwords like 'local', 'small batch' and 'hand crafted' became favoured across the food and drink industry and any booze production that reflected this had a natural edge in the battle for the hipster vote. The trend winds favoured gin, even if it didn't know it yet.

With regards to the second factor, throughout history whenever cocktails are popular, so too is gin. The 1860s to the turn of the 1900s saw a cocktail era that glittered with some of the most iconic bar books ever written (*Jerry Thomas' Bar Tenders Guide* being the best known, written in 1862). Following the First World War and during the 1920s, cocktails were back in vogue. In both eras are the origins of gin cocktail recipes that have stood the test of time (the Tom Collins and the French 75 to name just two). Each time that cocktail culture is on a high, it seems that gin, a versatile botanical spirit, is a key member of the bartender's arsenal.

In the noughties, speakeasy-themed bars inspired by elements of those eras began to emerge once more, first opening in the USA, then thriving in cities all over the world. Milk & Honey, PDT and Pegu Club changed the definition of a New York cocktail bar, as well as the general attitude of those working in the drinks industry and what consumers wanted to drink.

Following their lead, over time fewer and fewer bars relied on their soda guns and pre-mixed syrups and menus featuring more historic recipes made with traditional mixing techniques started to appear elsewhere. Unsurprisingly, in the search for authentically recreated recipes ignited by the re-birth of the modern cocktail movement, gin made its natural return to the liquor rails and rose in popularity.

The Internet Effect

It is easy to forget how computer illiterate the world was, even as recently as the year 2000. Facebook was invented in 2004 . . . Twitter in 2006 . . . Having individual brand websites, let alone an active consumer database, was rare for most drinks brands until at least 2008. Global conversation around trends did not play out as it does today and a bartender-led movement in New York, for example, may never have caught on elsewhere without the internet showcasing it. Within years, previously separated and sometimes isolated communities were sharing notes and taking cues from one another.

Small producers benefited too. They could reach new fans and build dedicated communities without their gins being available to buy outside their country of origin. Gin fans could more easily discover new brands and their expectations were raised. The quality and the authenticity of a distiller's story prevailed over lavish advertising campaigns. From very little ability to access information, there was now a thirst for it, and the need to present it in the best possible light was clear for all to see. The iconic Beefeater Gin Master distiller, Desmond Payne MBE, summed it up neatly when he said, 'We were just known as Distillery managers back then, now we are Master distillers.'

BOOM FROM BUST

While changing laws, early pioneers, global cocktail trends and the rise of the internet all played a role in the rise of modern gin, we want to touch on a final factor best represented by a simple statistic: over 75% of craft distilleries active in the USA, UK and Australia today were set up after 2009.

We don't credit the 2008 banking crisis as the instigator for a movement, there was clearly a growing trend by that point as we have previously discussed, but there is a correlation between the banking crisis occurring and craft distilling dramatically increasing.

We are not suggesting that the cash taps were suddenly opened to small distilling businesses, but investors were seeking out alternative opportunities that once had seemed risky and, after 2008, the craft distilling industry seemed notably less risky. Bulldog Gin was created in 2007 by a former banker, Anshuman Vohra. Jensen's Gin was launched by Christian Jensen in 2005–2006, also in investment banking. While both of these independents launched before the crisis, by 2010, neither looked like the folly they might have seemed before.

Another indirect consequence of the banking crisis was, for some, a need to seek alternative employment. A surprising amount of early craft distillers came directly out of businesses that had been adversely affected by the banking collapse. Sacred Gin founder Ian Hart, for example, felt it was the time to pursue his dream, launching in 2009. The same impetus was felt by Miko Abouaf who changed career to begin his journey into distilling (later creating Pink Pepper Gin), while for many others, the seeds were also being sown. Gin Foundry as a company was, incidentally, an idea that took form directly due to this changed landscape. From disaster was born entrepreneurialism.

In terms of the consumer, and what they preferred to drink, the crash encouraged drinkers to shun big brands in favour of 'honest', 'authentic' local alternatives and for bars to stock greater choice to meet this demand. As Jimmy Carter slammed the 'Three Martini Lunch' to illustrate his point about unfair taxes during the 1976 Presidential campaign, magnums of vodka and Champagne spraying were vilified in the media as displays of the banking elite's arrogance. At the very least subconsciously, craft gin was the humble alternative!

The consumer appreciation of the craftsmanship involved in making spirits had leaped forward in only a few years, and none of that would have been possible without the wake up call and anti-big business sentiment that the recession triggered. Early craft distillers were no longer considered on the fringes and 'craft' distilling was associated with a credence, authenticity and wholesomeness it could not have attained without the events of the previous few years.

CRAFT GOES GLOBAL

With the explosion of small distilleries in the US and the UK, it is all too easy to forget that it took well into the 2010s before any smaller, micro-distiller broke through to become a globally recognised craft gin brand. Craft gin may have been thriving in connoisseur, hipster and bartender circles, but it wasn't on the radar of the average consumer yet.

From the USA, 209 Gin, Junípero, Leopold's and Bluecoat were gaining momentum, but with no big distribution breakthroughs they never really created global momentum. FEW Spirits, Aviation, Death's Door and St George were also successful, and growing nationally, but were not big enough to produce the volumes needed to meet global commercial demand for a while.

In the UK, brands like Sipsmith and William Chase grew alongside the other independents, but the now-recognised craft distillers of Edinburgh Gin, Warner Edwards or Adnams didn't even exist until 2010 onwards and took years to gain traction. Elsewhere in the world, Monkey 47 and Four Pillars were enjoying the early attention of the curious, but weren't well-known brands until 2015. South African early adopter Inverroche (2012) is still under the radar internationally.

By 2015, all across the world, even small start-ups could just about afford to create a craft distillery. At first, new openings used stills that were just a touch smaller than 500 litre, in subsequent years small became smaller and some even open distilleries with stills as small as 20L today. Once the door had been opened, distiller after distiller added to, elevated and broadened craft distilling as an industry and with it gin has flourished as a category ever since.

In 2009, the UK had 30-odd distilleries. By 2018, it had over 300. From the 300 or so distilleries that were active around 2010 in the USA, in 2018 there were well over 1,500. In Australia, the small handful of distilleries has reached almost 80-strong.

Every country has its marquee names that helped build a local craft offering on the success of the big multinational players. Leopold Bros, Sipsmith, Four Pillars and Monkey 47 for example all changed the way the next generation looked at what was possible and in doing so, allowed the very idea of craft distilling to go from a small hobby industry to a global phenomenon.

GIN DRINKING TODAY

The French might have a 'paradox' when it comes to food, seemingly living the good life, eating foods rich in cholesterol and drinking wine, but without the subsequent mass onset of diabetes and obesity, but when it comes to gin it is the Philippines which is a veritable contradiction. Despite being one of the smallest importers of gin, the Philippines is the biggest per capita consumer. Not by a little either, but by such an extent that they usually have to be ignored in international statistics as not doing so skews the entire global picture.

Statistically, Filipinos drink the most per capita and over 100 million bottles of their leading brand, Ginebra San Miguel, are consumed almost entirely locally. Astonishingly, this figure (equivalent to over 40% of gin consumed globally each year) is more than Gordon's and Tanqueray make and sell to the rest of the world combined. Given its huge success, it may come as a surprise that to taste, it is not a particularly unusual or even a strikingly good gin either. There's a certain sweetness to the nose, but there's enough juniper to pass it off as classically styled. Its forte is its ability to be a please-all flavour and therein lies its success.

Gin is so firmly embedded in Filipino culture that it has strong symbolic roles too, to the extent that when a new bottle is opened a shot of gin is often either poured on the floor to share with ancestral spirits, or consumed in their honour.

The Spanish drink the second most gin per capita, in their fish bowl-sized copa glasses, which are their preferred way of drinking G&Ts. So attached are they to the humble G&T that Madrid and Barcelona can comfortably lay claim to being the capitals of the drink, a moniker they both take seriously, with some ostentatious combinations being the norm when it comes to how best to garnish the drink.

In stark contrast to the Philippines, most of the gin brands available are imported. It is the biggest export market for British gin within the EU, with Beefeater Gin the largest booze brand of any category across Spain.

Per capita consumption aside, the title for second biggest market by volume goes to America. Americans may drink less gin per head than many countries, some 0.2 litres (7 fl oz) per capita, but by volume enough gin is sunk in bars and restaurants to make the USA a formidable consumer.

Due to the reasonably low tax duty on alcohol, both American gins and brands exported there (the US accounted for 59% of non-EU exports of British gin in 2016) tend to be higher proof, averaging between 45% to 48% ABV as the standard strength. Survey after survey also show that the US is unusual in that the gin and tonic is much less popular than elsewhere around the world, with the Martini and the Negroni performing much stronger by comparison to any other country.

Rising markets such as South Africa and Australia have grown at a rapid pace since 2015 and are making up for lost time. Arriving late to the craft distilling movement is serving them well, as so far it is clear that they have seen the lessons learned elsewhere and are fast becoming the source for many of the most exciting, diverse and globally minded brands to break into the category. Meanwhile, all eyes look to Japan and South America as both show signs of a resurgence that could see them become major consumers and producers of the next generation of global brands from 2020 onwards.

The UK, despite its historic importance in gin making, is neatly tucked into the middle of the pile on almost every conceivable stat relating to consumption, perceptions and trends. The UK stands behind the likes of Slovakia and the Netherlands on per capita consumption, with the average Brit drinking 0.5 litres (17 fl oz) of gin per year compared to the Slovak's 1.2 litres (42 fl oz) and Dutch 0.7 litres (24 fl oz).

By overall volume consumed nationally, the UK ranks third behind the US and Spain with a preference for how to drink gin also lying somewhere in between the two, favouring the G&T, but with a growing love of the Negroni.

Yet, it is not with a false or outdated sense of grandness that the UK considers itself the epicentre of the gin category. The UK exerts a huge global influence on the category today, with new ideas, flavour trends and ways to consume it emerging from the country. Dozens of new distillers are taught at the famous Heriot-Watt University on their Brewing and Distilling degree course each year, while even more individuals travel to enroll onto shorter courses at the Institute of Brewing and Distilling annually. Few other countries have anything similar in terms of education for apprentice ginsmiths and because of this, many overseas attendees adopt British ways of working and take their learnings with them, further propagating trends that emanate in the UK. There are Livery Companies for distillers and Guilds for gin makers actively promoting and championing gin on governmental trade and diplomatic levels too. Nowhere else is there such infrastructure for the spirit to grow and for local distillers' ideas about how to make it to be passed onto others.

And lets not forget the UK-born powerhouse heritage brands of Gordon's, Bombay Sapphire and Tanqueray, three of the biggest brands in the world, who have exported gin to the most obscure of places around the globe and sell over 146 million bottles between them every year (incidentally, that's three times what the UK drinks annually). Beefeater is edging towards the 'top three' listing, with Hendrick's and Sipsmith not far behind, showing just how big British gin making is by volume too.

HOW GIN IS MADE

There are dozens of methods used to create gin and numerous kinds of apparatus employed in modern gin production in order to distil and extract the desired flavours.

For the most part, gin makers begin with a highly rectified neutral base alcohol, typically derived from wheat, potato, barley, grape, molasses or sugar cane.

Less than 15% make their own base spirit and, while this is a growing area of the category and one we would love to see more of (as it adds many layers to the process that are fun to write about and observe), it is uncommon due to being expensive and time consuming. To understand why so few do it or why some do not see it as part of the craft of making a gin, one must understand that the role of gin maker is slightly different to that of a vodka producer. It is an artform that is more about creating flavours from a vast array of botanicals than it is about creating smooth alcohol from an agricultural product. For many gin makers, the base is a canvas and what is painted upon that spirit, the botanicals, is the most important part.

Some gin makers will compound their recipes, which means they steep the botanicals or essences in the base spirit then filter them out ahead of bottling. This involves no distillation and can be seen in the likes of American-made Uncle Val's Gin, who employ this technique to brilliant effect, in particular to retain the vivid fresh nature of cucumber (which is so crisp it's as if one has been snapped in half under your nose). Sometimes this kind of gin is called bathtub gin, a nod to the Prohibition era where this method was used more frequently.

For those who distil, the two most frequently used techniques are to macerate or to vapour infuse – sometimes both at the same time! Those who macerate their botanicals place the ingredients in the pot of the still along with the neutral spirit. This can be done just before the distillation occurs, but sometimes it happens up to 48 hours before, and each maker's fiercely guarded recipe will call for a very specific way of treating the botanicals and the duration for which they are steeped (i.e. macerated). A classic example of this is Beefeater Gin, who macerate their botanicals for 24 hours ahead of distilling their London Dry Gin.

Those who vapour infuse place their botanicals in a chamber high up the still rather than in the pot and the ingredients do not come into contact with the base spirit until distillation is underway. In this method, as the alcohol vapour starts to rise up the still, it arrives at the vapour chamber and passes through the botanicals (similar to the idea of steaming something). The alcohol vapour picks up their flavour and, once clear of the chamber, is re-condensed into liquid. Bombay Sapphire is the most famous example of a gin that is made using vapour extraction.

Some distillers, equipped with stills that have the capacity to do both, macerate some botanicals, and place others in the vapour chamber. By using both techniques, they are seeking to process the botanicals in the most favourable way. For example, Dartmouth Gin place lavender, rose and rosemary in the vapour chamber (alongside others) to ensure they only have a gentle heat applied to them, while their core flavours of juniper and grains of paradise are derived from those botanicals being steeped overnight and placed in the heart of their still. The result combines the robust nature of one method with the lightness of touch of the other and their gin is, as a result, deliciously fresh and light, yet satisfyingly juniper forward and resinous to taste.

Gin making, just as with everything else, has embraced new ideas and new technology. Some gin makers use a method that is known as 'vacuum distilling' or 'cold distilling', which means the atmospheric pressure inside of the still is removed, creating a vacuum, which reduces the temperature required for ethanol to distil. This is typically done on glass stills but, more and more, there are big copper stills that have the capacity to do this.

Due to the lower temperatures being applied, the flavours extracted from the botanicals taste different – for example, vacuum distilled citrus offers a fresher, brighter note compared to the more rounded, caramelised notes of traditional distilling. Which style is preferred is subjective, but what is clear is that new methods, such as vacuums, are unlocking flavours that have not been available before and are helping gin flourish in a new era and evolve alongside modern drinkers' expectations.

BOTANICAL LEGALITIES

When it comes to making gin there is one rule that matters above all others – to have gin you must have juniper. This only stipulation was enshrined into the EU law in 2008: 'that the taste is predominantly that of juniper'. The equivalent US Federal legalities (which have been updated over the years) also state that gin 'shall derive its main characteristic flavour from juniper berries'.

How much juniper is enough to pass as 'predominant' has been debated for decades. Some argue that the category has moved at such speed that gin can't, for better and for worse, be restricted by the rules that were set so long ago, while a blatant disregard by some gin makers to ensure they have evident juniper in their gin has ruffled many feathers over the years.

No brand to date has been removed from shelves due to a lack of juniper, and there has been no real policing of the rules either. In our opinion, it is impossible to reverse the tide of botanical spirits that now call themselves gin as a result.

On a positive note though, thanks to the lack of enforcement and the immensely versatile nature of how botanicals can combine in gin, we can now enjoy a kaleidoscope of flavour. There are literally hundreds of botanicals, along with juniper, that can be used to make excellent gins, with thousands of possible iterations. Even the slightest tweak to dosages of the same ingredient list can create entirely different results. Gin as a category would never have become as big if it were not for those looking to push boundaries of 'juniperiness', or had innovation and experimentation of new flavours not become central to modern makers.

Juniper aside, it is worth noting that there are some botanicals that cannot be used in certain parts of the world, which is why some gins are not exported everywhere. For example, botanicals such as meadowsweet or tonka are not permitted for gins destined for the USA, as the ingredients also give off compounds (in minute amounts) that the government considers to be dangerous. In the case of the two botanicals mentioned, alongside their beautiful flavours, you can also extract coumarin, which has blood-thinning properties, while the likes of willow bark contains salicin, from which you can derive aspirin. In the rest of the world, you can quaff TOAD Gin (meadowsweet) or drink Patient Wolf Gin (tonka) freely because legislators understand that to get the adverse effects, one would have to drink well over a litre of gin. If you are doing this, the side-effects of one botanical component are the least of your worries.

Juniper

If you want to really understand gin, it's important to know juniper. We would compare it to understanding the influence of casks for whisk(e)y fans or grapes for oenophiles.

Juniper shrubs vary in size and shape, are evergreen and are usually low spreading bush-type plants. The 'berries' are, technically, pine cones, and they can vary quite dramatically in size depending on where they are grown and how old they are. There is no other way to harvest juniper berries than by hand and harvest time involves pickers with big bags and sticks gently beating down the bushes in a procession that is still similar to what it might have been in the Middle Ages. As a botanical, juniper is used in dozens of herbal tinctures too, including in Scandinavian beers and in numerous Italian vermouths.

Most of the global supply of juniper for the gin industry comes from Macedonia and Tuscany, although there are more producers emerging from other regions (such as Croatia and Bulgaria in Europe or Vermont and Oregon in the US), where the juniper is being sustainably harvested and used more prevalently.

Scottish Highland and Scandinavian juniper are other micro-regions used by local gin makers to superb effect. This has been taken to extremes by the likes of Crossbill Gin, who famously produced a batch of gin from a single bush! Loch Ness Gin forages around the fabled Scottish loch for their botanicals, including juniper, meaning their production is restricted to just a few thousand bottles a year. Meanwhile, Northumbria-made Hepple Gin uses Italian juniper alongside greener local English juniper to marry the piny nature of one with the green, grassy nature of the other.

Just like grapes, each crop of juniper is affected differently by the sun, soil and the climactic conditions in which it grows (you'll see some of this 'terroir' highlighted in gin marketing). Gin Mare is one such gin, which uses some Mediterranean juniper and states that the added heat and sunshine the crop has to endure brings a much richer, oily mouthfeel to their gin.

Most brands will not specify their juniper's provenance, however, as they make their juniper selection based on the specific flavour profiles they desire and the quality they seek, as opposed to their geography. Depending on the distiller's criteria, this means the location where the juniper is grown will vary over the years as the aim is to produce a consistent product, meaning they have to be flexible with location in order to be rigid with recipe requirements.

For the variety of juniper (there are over 40), almost all gin makers use *Juniperus communis*, selecting regional flavour differences as opposed to a completely different variety. A notable exception to this is Procera Gin from Kenya, which is named after the nuttier and earthier juniper variety *Juniperus procera*, which they use in conjunction with the regular *communis*.

WHAT TO LOOK FOR WHEN CHOOSING GIN

No one falls into an existential crisis when shopping for gin, worrying about what's inside the bottle to the point of simply freezing in the middle of the aisle overwhelmed by choice, nor does anyone Google each one to check out multiple critics' reviews before picking the right one for them. There will be certain factors and terms that make a bigger impact on your decisions than others, however, and it's good to arm yourself with some understanding of the context that surrounds them. Knowing these simple things will help you make a more informed decision, and prevent you from being bamboozled into believing any old spin laid on by a clever wordsmith.

DECIPHERING GIN LABELS

Gin labels don't enjoy the same formalities as wine labels. There is no template, no standardised way of saying what's inside and, actually, very little in terms of consistent language (which is the frustrating thing about the aforementioned juniper dosage disagreements, as most people don't mind variety, but some do like to know what to expect from what they are buying!).

Here are some common phrases that do appear and what they mean:

ABV

This stands for alcohol by volume. The minimum for gin in the UK is 37.5% (40% in the US and 43% in South Africa), so anything under that is either a liqueur or illegal. Gins can go as high as they want, with the most we've ever encountered (that wasn't a pure gimmick) being Swedish gin Strane, with their 'Uncut' version bottled at a whopping 76% ABV, but on average the majority of gins are between 40 and 45%.

Location

The location on a label may have nothing to do with where the distillery is based, or where the botanicals come from. Gins named after cities, lakes or landscapes can be made anywhere and they don't even need to grow or forage botanicals in that area. For example 'Japanese' gin can be made in the UK, just as 'Bristol' gin can be made in Spain. While most gins will have strong links between the statement of provenance and the actual location of the distillery, it isn't a requirement. There's no need for investigative journalism at each and every purchase though – almost all will celebrate their maker's locations with authenticity, but it's worth remembering this fact, as there are always some who take advantage of this marketing tool and try to imply a false sense of identity. Read the wording carefully as the devil is always in the detail!

London Dry Gin

Sometimes used colloquially to describe archetypal, classic, juniper forward flavours, when seen on a label this is a term used to state that the liquid meets a certain set of distillation requirements set out in EU law. Because of this, when a label says London Dry, remember it is about production, not place nor flavour. For example, amongst many others, the rules state the minimum ABV of the distilled alcohol flowing from the still, as well as such matters as the flavour must be entirely derived through distillation and that no further flavourings, essences or infusions can be added post distillation (London Dry cannot be coloured), and only a minute amount of sweetener (defined in very specific terms) is allowed.

Small batch

The term is not regulated and there is no consensus as to what constitutes a 'small' batch. Many gins that display the term produce 20,000 bottles or more at a time, while others with the same tag make less than 80 bottles per distillation run. While one is ludicrously high and the other best described as hobby-sized, for the sake of clarity in our descriptions (and perhaps as a way of demonstrating there is a reasonable middle ground), we regard a small batch as being less than 2,000 bottles of finished gin per distillation run. Some small batch gins number their bottles so you can get a sense of scale, while emerging terms in the industry that might help in years to come are 'micro' and 'nano'.

It can be misleading to see the size of a still and assume that it only makes tiny batches. It is possible to turbo-charge a recipe and create such a concentrated distillate that you can add up to 30 times the amount of bulk ethanol to it afterwards, before cutting with water to bottling strength. In employing this procedure, producers use a medium-sized 500 litre (132 US gallon) still to create a whopping 20,000 bottles per batch or even more. This 'multi-shot' process (sometimes called concentrate), instead of the 'one-shot' process, is not necessarily a bad thing though. The makers don't create a balanced product and then thin it down with a more neutral spirit; they create a turbo-charged distillate that needs alcohol added to it in order for it to taste as intended, similar to the idea of using food extracts in baking. The recipe is deliberately concentrated so that it is best used in small amounts and the flavours expand when diluted.

Moreover, only a tiny minority who use this multi-shot technique add anywhere near 20 times as much fluid after. There are hundreds of fantastic distillers who use the multi-shot methodology only adding two to three times more neutral alcohol to keep it small, controlled and with a rich mouthfeel, producing world-class gins. The process merely allows them to increase their capacity a little and reduce the cost of their bottles for the end consumer. As an example, Campfire Navy Strength Gin is one such product, where the balance between botanical intensity and overall impact is carefully measured for a phenomenal effect that's the best of both worlds.

Handcrafted and craft gin

As you've probably guessed by now, these terms, too, are not regulated. Any gin could technically be considered a 'craft gin'. It's important to note that just because something is made by either a conglomerate or a multinational company does not mean it is not made by a genuinely handcrafted, artisanal process. For example, Bombay Sapphire's care and diligence in their botanicals selection and their purchasing ethics, along with their distillery's environmental policy and their production process, make a compelling case for it being a craft gin.

Some drinkers state that craft gin can't be made by a third-party contractor who distils the gin on a brand owner's behalf, others will say that the distillery that produces it must produce under a certain volume per year, irrespective of batch size. Some say it's because something is 'done by hand'. All of these are good points, if flawed when considered in isolation of other factors. The first two ignore process altogether, and to our knowledge, no human can distil alcohol using their hands alone. Conversely, no distillery (even Ginebra San Miguel – producer of over a hundred million bottles in the Philippines), has automated the process as to not need humans to measure the botanicals and run the distillery. To decide whether something is handcrafted or not, it is important to see the entire picture and to judge the gin in the spirit in which it is made. You need to balance ownership, process, scale and automation with fair importance in order to come up with an overall assessment.

If you are specifically looking for a small, local gin maker, look for clear, simultaneous multiple indicators – distillery location, batch size and information about the distillation process.

Gluten free

ALL distilled gin is gluten free. Distillation is the process of separating out alcohol and gluten can't travel with ethanol vapour, so there is no way that it could be found in the resulting distillate. 'Gluten free' might seem reassuring to some, but it is not a unique selling point.

Other observations

If the liquid has any tint to it, it was either made by a compound method or it has been infused or aged *after* distillation. Almost all of these factors will be explained on a label, but it is worth knowing so that you can instantly get an indication of what to expect and clues as to how it has been made.

TASTING GIN

Gin may be clear to the eye but contained within is a multitude of compounds that form a complex chemistry poised to deliver moments of pure pleasure. Essential oils that have been extracted from each botanical through the process of distillation each have their distinct flavours.

Juniper gives off big doses of alpha-Pinene with its woody pine intensity; citrus peels deliver limonene with its clear, zesty twang; coriander seeds provide swathes of linalool, bringing in a lemony, sometimes slightly floral touch; and roots such as angelica bring with them terpine compounds such as humulene, with its earthy, musty and sometimes stale notes. Of course, all botanicals will have multiple combinations of these, in varying levels of intensity – all of which conspire to make balancing a recipe incredibly hard work. Moreover, these are just a few botanicals and a few of the compounds that make up gin's spectacular array of flavours.

Each compound will have a different volatility (some fly off at the first opportunity, others take a while to get going and become noticeable to the nose or palate), which is why no gin has a flavour that occurs all at once. Gin's flavour must always be considered as an evolving journey through time, not a single note delivered in a single moment.

Citrus botanicals tend to have more compounds that are higher in volatility, while spice and roots tend to be laden with much lower ones, which means that citrus tends to burst off the top of the glass while spice and roots tend to become apparent towards the finish of a sip. In perfume, the order in which scents are perceived is often described as 'top notes', 'heart notes' and 'base notes' and the same is true of gin, where there is a clear order to a flavour journey.

There are botanicals that are used as the peak of a flavour arc, the obvious 'notes' so to speak (such as juniper, which most gin makers want to ensure is apparent in the flavour journey), while others bridge flavours from one to the next. Some botanicals are perennially used in small dosages to underpin proceedings and add a weight without ever becoming palpable. Consider them the shade, which sets off the intensity and shine of the star botanical by contrast. For example, cracked pepper can anchor a gin's profile, allowing drinkers to better perceive just how intense the likes of a citrus peel-like yuzu can be on the nose. One is more obvious because the other contrasts it, even if it may not be evident at first or in its own right.

As drinkers, you do not need to be scientifically minded to be able to experience this. To taste a gin, pour it into a wine glass, taste it twice and take your time.

First Tasting

Pour some gin into a glass without mixer or ice.

Smell it ('the nose')

What does it smell of? What's the overall impression and is there a lead note you can detect? Is it spirity or botanically intense? Does it leap out at you or draw you in? Does it evoke a memory and what does the impression remind you of?

Taste it ('the palate')

What's the first impression and then what arrives next? What's the mouthfeel like?

Assess the finish

What's the enduring sensation? How long does it last? Does it burn or is it smooth?

Second Tasting

This time, add a dash of water to 'cut' the gin. Certain botanicals are more evident after a dash of water is added, much like when tasting whisk(e)y. This is because lower volatile compounds tend to be more water-soluble (hydrophilic), and so changing the alcohol level will change the chemistry in your glass, as well as the perceived intensity of the ingredients.

Ask yourself how has it changed? Which notes are more prominent and is there anything that was underlying that has now become clearer? And vice versa, has anything disappeared from the profile?

The two-stage approach will help you experience the full spectrum of flavours contained in each drop and give you a good indication of what kind of a garnish might be appropriate to accentuate, complement or contrast with the gin when it comes to making a G&T.

A good tip is to hold the gin in your mouth for several seconds before swallowing. Hold it there for longer than you think is appropriate and for at least five seconds! It will feel alien as a process, but the nuances will reveal themselves better as your mouth desensitises to the ABV and your tastebuds adjust accordingly.

Describing What You Can Taste

It may seem surprising, but even at the highest level of the spirits industry there is a lack of confidence when it comes to expressing aroma and taste. Distillers, critics, bartenders and 'connoisseurs' know what they like and can recognise flavours better than most because they habitually taste spirits. Yet, despite this, many will avoid sharing tasting notes. There isn't yet an oenophile equivalent in the spirit industry.

The best entry point is to describe a gin in four parts: the aroma, the taste, the finish and the overall impression. Try and be precise with the first three and a little more whimsical with the last (what did it taste like, not what did it taste of).

Try and use all the descriptive words at your disposal, including any that may be more familiar for colours, or even shapes, that the gin might inspire in your mind, as well as what you can taste or smell.

For example, tonka, nutmeg, almonds and other aromas/flavours that have a patisserie-like feel to them tend to be reminiscent of amber, honey tones or rich and enveloping shades of brown. Floral notes can be described in a variety of shades of rosy pink, red and yellow, just like the real thing. Ask yourself if what you taste is vivid or dull, or perhaps light or dark? In doing so, you'll start to get some words that you can build on.

There are many parallels between a flavour journey and describing forms too, with ways to draw similarities between sharp angles, undulating flavours, increasingly crescent intensities and more. Whether something has a rounded flavour, a circular nature or if it plateaus after a certain point or tapers off dramatically. These words can be helpful when looking at ways to bridge between the specificity of the flavour and the impression or duration for which it lasts. Touch and texture work for some, sounds work for others. There is no right and wrong, so feel confident in owning the vocabulary that works for you.

Don't forget that it doesn't need to always be about labelling the exact botanical either, it can both be easier and more effective to describe what something feels like generally, as opposed to what it literally is. For example, a flavour that's reminiscent of key lime pie is more vivid a description than saying it tastes of lime peel (assuming that's what you are trying to describe!).

Just like a painting, each gin will have a character and a 'feeling' about it, from relaxed to hyper-charged. Some will leave you mellow while others will be bursting with bright happiness. That emotive quality is something that can be useful to tap into when describing gin as, often, it is in the more whimsical summaries that the most visceral and engaging descriptions can emerge.

An ideal blind tasting to showcase the contrast in flavours and the full spectrum of moods would be something like this: Death's Door Gin brings with it a sense of calm and of the American Midwest alongside warming fennel; Australian Distillery Botanica Gin and South African Inverroche have numerous gins that are laden with the mystique of their respective country's flora and depict a colourful scene between them (one is luscious and green, the other a haze of summery, buttery yellows); Surrey-made Copperfield London Dry Gin brings British history to life using an old recipe found in archives dating back to 1750 and reimagined for the modern drinker; Ferdinand's Saar Dry Gin, on the other hand, brings with it a unique flinty minerality that has you questioning the similarities between viniculture and gin making (as well as asking for more). All have different personalities, with different intensities, some of which will be instantly emotive, others more cerebral, requiring contemplation and context to fully understand.

Context is key when it comes to gin, and it is worth trying to remember two further things as you go on your voyage of discovery:

1. The entirety of the flavours in gin are chosen and made by a distiller. There's no alchemy of time or the mysticism of years spent in a cellar, as with wine or whisk(e)y. How a gin tastes is the result of a maker's touch and their creative vision. Keeping the distillers and where the gin is made geographically in mind is important when trying to understand a gin, as it often provides context as to why something tastes the way it does and can help provide insight into how something is made.

2. It is just gin, there's no need for navel gazing and obnoxious snobbery. Taste it to discover what you like and dislike; how you prefer to drink it. Then relax, pour a double, get the ice, tonic perhaps, and just enjoy it.

Botanical Tasting Wheel

ACIDIC
SOUR
ZESTY
JUICY
FLESHY
CLEAN
CRISP
RIPE
TANGY
JAMMY
PLUMP
CANDIED
STEWED
AROMATIC
FRESH
PERFUMED
FRAGRANT
CALMING
VERDANT
LEAFY

CITRUSY
FRUITY
BERRIES
FLORAL
GRASSY

Buddha's Hand
Bergamot
Lemon Aspen
Lemon
Mandarin
Yuzu
Grapefruit
Pomelo
Bitter Orange
Sweet Orange
Pineapple
Mango
Quandong
Apricot
Nectarine
Peach
Baobab
Melon
Cantaloupe
Cucumber
Kiwi
Apple
Sea Buckthorn
Quince
Greengage
Pear
Mirabelle Plum
White Mulberry
Fig
Grape
Physalis
Gooseberry
Rowan Berry
Redcurrant
Lingonberry
Raspberry
Strawberry
Cherry
Elderberry
Blackberry
Blackcurrant
Rhubarb
Raspberry Leaf
Wild Rosella
Hibiscus
Rosehip
Rose
Violet
Lavender
Jasmine
Geranium
Iva Flower
Butterfly Pea Flower
Honeysuckle
Edelweiss
Tilia
Bee Balm
Honey Bush
Honey Myrtle
Marigold
Osmanthus
Chamomile
Gorse
Elderflower
Lemon Balm
Lemon Thyme
Linden
Lemon Myrtle
Lemon Verbena
Kaffir Lime Leaf
Pineapple Weed
Sorrel
Woodruff
Meadowsweet
Yarrow
Hyssop
Fennel
Celery Seed

GIN STYLES

Gin is a vast global category with as many idiosyncrasies as it has flavours. We are spoilt for choice, as are barkeeps curating which gins to stock and how best to serve them. Even the most traditional of British pub will now serve a number of gins (if only one tonic). For those fighting over *The Guinness Book of Records* title for best-stocked gin bar, you'll need over 1,200 to even be in the race . . .

The rise of gin is, in some ways, comparable to that of craft beer, which has also exploded in the past two decades. Both have seen a huge expansion in the amount of styles and the number of producers that have emerged. Even though there are similarities, a better comparison for gin is the perfume industry's parallel growth and its parallel trends.

Older generations of perfume consumers had a tendency to wear one or two specific brands and stick to them throughout their lives, while today's fragrance enthusiasts have several and are far less loyal to one perfume house. This is identical to gin and modern purchasing habits surrounding it. Just as with gin, some releases are seasonal, some are limited editions, some are a special treat and some are for everyday use. Gin has called its flavour differences 'styles', while the perfume industry has tailored its scents towards specific 'audiences'. Each respective industry has real heritage brands, as well as those who falsely appropriate it for their marketing and new disruptive entrants turning category assumptions on their head.

The parallels are almost identical and while the comparisons can go on and on, the most remarkable similarity is that to succeed in either category, brands need to have the perfect balance of a compelling narrative matched with stylish packaging and contents that can stir the senses.

With this in mind, you can start looking for what to buy by becoming familiar with broader 'styles' of gin and note down some of the amazing brands within each and how best to serve them.

We've split the gin category into six styles. We start with Classic (juniper forward dry gins), then go to Contemporary (more subdued juniper and more prominently noticeable other botanicals), as these form the majority of gins available in the world today.

We then delve into the sub-styles, such as the boozy Navy Strength gins, the historical Old Tom genre, the increasingly popular Cask-aged gins and the recent trend for Fruit-infused Gins and Gin Liqueurs.

CLASSIC GINS

It is important to reiterate here that the term London Dry Gin doesn't always mean a classic gin flavour. London Dry is often misused as a term to describe classic flavours because they often go together, but London Dry is actually a statement of production not flavour, so it is possible to get very adventurous, progressive flavours made to London Dry standards (see Deciphering Gin Labels page 25).

To appreciate what it is to be a classically styled gin, one must first look to the brands that have stood the test of time, as it is their flavour profiles that are considered 'traditional' gin today. These heritage brands share a few things in common botanically as well as the methods they use to distil. It is even possible to see the influence of trade routes and colonisation in classic gins, when botanicals became available and fashionable and which regions offered the best ingredients at the time these distilleries first emerged.

Classic gin botanicals include spices from Morocco – mainly coriander seeds – and from further along what was known as the Pepper Coast (the present-day area that covers Sierra Leone, the Ivory Coast and Liberia) grains of paradise were exported in huge quantities. So much so, that by 1880 the *Encyclopædia Britannica* was reporting, 'Grains of paradise are to some extent used in veterinary practice, but for the most part illegally to give a fictitious strength to malt liquors, gin, and cordials.' Cassia, cinnamon and nutmeg are also prevalent in historic recipes brought back from Sri Lanka and Indonesia.

The use of dried peels, as opposed to fresh citrus, is important to note in classic gin making. Prior to the 1850s, ships could not bring in fresh supplies at a cheap enough price point for most distillers, so the dried peels of bitter Seville oranges, for example, were more frequently used in traditional recipes over the fresh Valencia oranges used by modern ginsmiths. Classic gins sometimes have no citrus at all, instead using the combination of juniper and coriander seeds – with coriander seed giving that desirable citrus twang. You can sample this in the likes of Tanqueray London Dry Gin, where the combination of the two (and the lack of citrus) is easy to discern.

To understand the flavours of traditional recipes and classic gins, don't be put off trying the big commercial brands. It would be like trying to be an architect having never come across Romanesque classicism, the Baroque movement or the Renaissance due to a reluctance to see the sights. To appreciate just how people have broken the rules with stunning effect, one must first understand the core of the category and the rules of thumb that have defined it.

Here are some of our favourites and a selection of classically styled gins that we think every drinker should know and have tasted for themselves. Tasting all four gins will help you understand the essence of a classic gin. Juniper is at the centre, with juniper and coriander seeds working in tandem in a pivotal role, driving the flavour. There will be warming citrus upfront if there is any, and warming spice at the back, followed by a dry finish.

Gordon's London Dry Gin

Such is the ubiquity of Gordon's that it is impossible not to have come across it. Gordon's was started in a Southwark-based distillery in London in 1769 by Alexander Gordon. Production later moved further east to Clerkenwell in 1786 and the spirit was exported from the early 1800s, creating legions of fans globally.

Gordon's is now distilled in various locations around the world and the exact botanical blend is kept undeclared. This London Dry Gin recipe is fiercely guarded, but allegedly contains juniper berries, coriander seeds, angelica root, liquorice, orrisroot, dried orange and lemon peel, ginger, cassia and nutmeg.

Affordable and excellent quality, Gordon's Gin is one of the original players and is also one of the world's first mass-produced quality gins, one that has stood the test of time. Have a look for it outside of the UK where it's bottled at a much stronger ABV of 47.5% and where that resinous juniper, coriander and cassia core is much more evident and the overall mouthfeel more luxurious than that of the UK's 37.5% ABV offering. Through tasting it, it is possible to experience what connoisseurs consider to be a 'classic gin structure'.

G&J Greenall's London Dry Gin

G&J Greenall's and Tanqueray both have gins that are a masterclass in how juniper can be accentuated by coriander seeds. They are two of the best gins to taste to understand just how the botanical duo work off each other. To successfully capture the story of either brand would require an entire book, maybe even an archive (both exist, respectively, for each distillery), but to understand their relevance today is thankfully much more straightforward.

Before Edward Greenall leased the Bridge Street distillery in Warrington in 1860 and established the G&J Greenall company name (the 'G' and 'J' being the initials of Edward Greenall's younger brothers Gilbert and John), Greenall's was a producer of affordable, decent gin, having been in operation for almost a century following its establishment by Thomas Dakin in 1761.

Under Edward Greenall's care, however, it became one of the most respected gin makers in the world. One of the oldest gins around today, Greenall's gin is a classic London Dry, containing eight different botanicals, including cassia bark, ground almonds, piny juniper and coriander seeds. It delivers exactly what you expect from something of that era – a robust, reliable and enjoyable gin.

Tanqueray London Dry Gin

Charles Tanqueray launched his distillery in the 1830s on Vine Street in Bloomsbury, London. It's thought that the Tanqueray gin recipe as we know it today first came about in 1838. The unchanging nature of the gin is an astonishing feat given how well balanced it is – even more so when one considers that Charles was a newbie distiller in his early twenties at the time.

When Charles Tanqueray died in 1868, his son (at the age of 20) inherited the distillery and continued his pioneering work. Under his guidance, the company grew and was exported to the British colonies. In 1898, Tanqueray merged with Gordon's & Company, cementing their place as a leading force in gin distilling ever since.

Tanqueray was distilled in London until the great air raid of 1941, when the London distillery was almost completely destroyed. Only one of the stills survived the bombing and this remaining still, known as 'Old Tom', now resides at Tanqueray's home in Cameron Bridge, Scotland.

The four botanicals thought to be used in Tanqueray (again, the recipe is technically a secret) are juniper, coriander seeds, angelica root and liquorice. They combine to create a smooth gin that's well balanced and with a juniper dominant taste. It is slightly drier than some other gins, but coriander adds both a touch of piquancy and hints of lemon on the nose.

Our favourite Tanqueray anecdote is a reminder of the era from which classic gin hails. The pineapple was a symbol of both hospitality and prosperity in the late 1700s and early 1800s. Pineapples were both very expensive and hard to get hold of given that they would rot before landing ashore, unless they were part of the cargo of the fastest and best ships the Navy had, so to own one and serve it to guests was very special. You'll see a pineapple, along with axes, on the bottle and in the Tanqueray family crest, as a nice reminder of gin's first glory days and their stature as a family.

Beefeater London Dry Gin

This gin can be traced back to 1863. Beefeater's 1876 company stock lists show a portfolio of gins with brand names such as Ye Old Chelsea Gin and James Burrough London Dry, as well as an 'Old Tom' style gin and a few others. Beefeater's was the product of experimentation by owner and founder James Burrough, blending a particular recipe of botanicals to create a bold, full-flavoured gin. It is also one of the earliest examples of a gin named after something other than the maker or the distillery in a move that can now be seen as a piece of marketing genius that was several decades ahead of its time.

Beefeater's enjoyed almost instant success and became the James Burrough Company's flagship product. The original Beefeater recipe book, dated 1895, specifies that nine botanicals are essential: juniper, angelica root, angelica seeds, coriander seeds, liquorice, almonds, orris root, Seville oranges and lemon peel. Production of Beefeater moved home in 1958 to Kennington, London, but the method of steeping and distilling devised by James Burrough remains virtually unchanged. It is the combination of method and botanicals that creates the big mouthfeel and flavour impact that's so distinct in this gin and defines the London Dry style to this day.

Beefeater's use of orange peel is key and it is that note, specifically, that you should familiarise yourself with as it is a recurrent theme in many newly made 'classic' gins.

MODERN CLASSIC GINS

Modern classics are only slightly different than the familiar household names mentioned in the previous section. We've separated the two sections out in order to be clearer on the timeline and to show that gins that have a classic style don't have to be old or from a different era. All of these modern classics were made after 2005. Moreover, many of these modern classics only change one or two things (be it botanical or in the distillation) to add a contemporary edge, while the overall structure remains comparable. To use the metaphor of architecture once more, it is like keeping the vernacular of historic buildings, but modernising them slightly to account for the era in which they now exist.

UK Gins

City of London Distillery's Christopher Wren Gin
This gin takes the classic construct of juniper, coriander and citrus, but adds a thicker layer of liquorice root to create a brilliant texture to the mouthfeel, giving it an enveloping sensation. While it might seem like a very modern departure in contrast with the overall impression of the gin itself, try this with a sliver of melon as a G&T garnish (or grapefruit peel if you don't feel brave enough).

Fifty Pounds Gin
This adds the herbal botanical winter savoury to bolster the verdant nature of juniper's heart. It's as archetypal as it comes and is one to discover if you enjoy a very clear, almost singular and unobstructed juniper note at the core of your flavour journey.

Portobello Road Gin
This adds a good dose of nutmeg to its classically styled botanical line up, which prolongs the finish and adds a warming tone that endures long after the final sip.

Hayman's London Dry Gin

This is a very similar construct to Beefeater, in which a
dried orange plays off a sticky juniper. It's not just the soft
citrus at the fore, nor the juniper delivery midway that's
worthy of praise, take note of angelica root's drying effect
on the finish here as it's noticeable (and delicious) in this gin.

6 O'clock Gin

This has a similar classical pedigree to the likes of Hayman's
or Bombay Dry Gin, but its focus is on a bright lemon peel
note to provide lift upfront. This slight change, not in the
type of botanical but in whether it is added fresh or dried,
gives it a lot more zing compared to the soft introduction
and more caramelised tones of Beefeater.

No.3 Gin

We think this is a gin everyone should try as it is built in a
classic way, yet maintains a clear sense of individuality with
the crafty use of fragrant cardamom and a bright zest of
fresh grapefruit. The use of both botanicals allow it to taste
both entirely new and completely familiar at the same time!
You can accentuate this further by using the same
combination as a dual garnish in a G&T too.

Sipsmith London Dry Gin

This brand combined all of gin's classical ideology in the
making of their gin. It is made using ten carefully selected
botanicals from around the globe: Macedonian juniper
berries, Bulgarian coriander seed, French angelica root,
Spanish liquorice root, Italian orrisroot, Spanish ground
almond, Chinese cassia bark, Madagascan cinnamon,
Seville orange peel and Spanish lemon peel (both dried). It
couldn't really be any truer to traditional London Dry Gin

(as was Sipsmith's intention). Sipsmith gin has strong notes of waxy juniper plus a definite citrus zing and a lingering depth. The cassia bark and cinnamon help add the typical warmth on the finish and the overall impression is that of a classically styled gin that is well rounded and smooth. This gin embodies the very idea of modern classic in that while it has a timeless flavour profile informed by the past, it was fully intended for a modern audience.

American Gins

American gins are often accused of being juniper shy, and as a generalisation they tend to be more citrus forward and subdued in how pronounced gin's signature botanical is. There are, however, absolute classics to be found across the country and a handful of brands that are arguably the epitome of classic gin, despite being produced by recently established distilleries with modern intentions.

Junípero Gin

Made by Anchor Distilling in Potrero Hill in California, you might be able to guess the predominant flavour profile of Junípero given its name! With pine forest like-tones, the gin combines a traditional juniper heart with a pronounced spiciness to finish. We like to think of it as the grandfather of classic American gin, not just as it was launched so far ahead of the curve in 1998, but because it's got an enduring presence and true character.

Big Gin

Launched in March 2012, Big Gin was the first product from Seattle-based distillery Captive Spirits, who have since added several barrel-aged editions to their range. The gin aged in peat casks is a rare treat that marries their flagship gin with that unique added layer of phenolic smoke that can only come from peat – with an enchanting effect. Allegedly, the name came from both the flavour profile of the gin as well as distiller Ben Capdevielle's nickname for his dad, Big Jim, himself a craft distiller in Wisconsin.

Big Gin has a relatively traditional botanical line-up with a definitive aroma and taste of juniper and grains of paradise spices throughout, accompanied by the ingenious modern use of Tasmanian pepper berry. This is a big, bold archetypal gin, but the reason we love it and why you need to try it, is because it so clearly shows just how much depth is possible while staying true to the idea of traditional flavour types.

Death's Door

This gin embodies the simple idea of harnessing the essence of juniper and merely complementing its complex flavour by using local botanicals that are grown within the state. Death's Door uses only three botanicals (juniper, coriander seeds and fennel) to sublime effect. All three parts are so clear to taste and one hands over to the next in a wondrous flavour journey, finishing on the soft anise-like warming tones of fennel. Try it with a sprig of mint and an orange peel in a G&T to really accentuate all of the flavours.

Barr Hill

Similarly minimal, Barr Hill only distils juniper through their custom-designed 300-gallon extraction still before adding honey afterwards. Despite the simplicity of the recipe, there is an amazingly complicated assault on the senses. Waxy flowers are so strong you can almost hear the buzz of the bees as they take the pollen. This is followed by strict, heavy juniper, which creates a luscious (almost sticky) pine forest note.

Australian Gins

Never Never Gin
Adelaide-based team Never Never took the approach to distil juniper three ways. They steep it in neutral spirit, they add fresh juniper in the pot just before distillation and they also add it into the vapour chamber. The impact (just like with Sipsmith who did the same with their V.J.O.P gin variant) is a three dimensional and intricate homage to the botanical and, while there are other botanicals that are used, this is a brilliant gin for those looking to understand just how multifaceted and complex juniper can be.

The Melbourne Gin Company Dry Gin
This has all the typical notes of classic gin, but cleverly uses macadamia nuts to increase the textural quality of the mouthfeel – in a similar way to how Greenall's or Beefeater use almond – making it ideal for a Martini. The gin is reflective of distiller Andrew Mark's background as a wine maker and showcases just how an understanding of structure (both flavour and textural in the way they present themselves and sit on the palate) is vital in any good gin.

McHenry Classic Dry Gin
Tasmanian-based McHenry Distillery doses in a gentle layer of warming star anise and fragrant cardamom spice to extend its flavour journey on the finish. The understated juniper does just enough to keep the star anise from running riot and it's this tension that is worth trying to

identify when tasted neat as it showcases the balance distillers have to achieve in order to be able to ensure the juniper core is present, but that it eventually dissipates to allow the spice to transition in. Try it with a lemon thyme garnish in a G&T to add an aromatic bouquet without getting in the way of the finish.

South African Gins

Hope on Hopkins London Dry Gin

Lemon peel works hard to acquaint itself with the nose, and while the first sip is a little sharp, the juniper and citrus come through well before mellowing into a surprising, but completely welcome, floral finish.

Six Dogs Karoo Gin

The line up of lemon buchu, Persian limes, mandarin or Acacia thorn tree and wild lavender may sound anything but classic gin, but they have been used with restraint, while the juniper is allowed to hold centre stage. It is the cunning marriage of the two and the subtlety with which locality is matched by classicism that makes Karoo Gin special. While it's the most progressive in this section, it helps showcase how it is possible to match modern aspirations around provenance with the heritage of the category.

European Gins

In the rest of Europe, there are numerous must-taste examples of modern classics, but the two we feel most passionately for (and one that ought to be in every cabinet across the world) are from Ireland and Germany.

Blackwater No.5

Founded by Peter Mulryan in 2014, Blackwater Distillery was one of the first in a new wave of craft distilleries opening in the Republic of Ireland and their flagship gin, Blackwater No.5, is as classic as the Parthenon in Greece. Blackwater No.5 Gin was designed from top to bottom using only the botanicals imported into Ireland by White's of Waterford, a spice merchant active during the nineteenth century.

Going through the company's archives, they found a treasure trove of botanicals once popular, but now overlooked: 'on the nose' cardamom notes mix with juniper and a faint lemon rind, leaving cracked pepper-like tones to emerge in an otherwise dusty mix. To taste, juniper appears alongside coriander seed, while warming spice from the cinnamon nips towards the end. There is huge depth to this gin, both in its flavour and its links to the area's heritage.

Elephant Gin

Crafted just outside of Hamburg, Elephant Gin is made up of 14 botanicals, none of which would suggest the classic style that it has: juniper and cassia bark, sweet orange peel, ginger, lavender, elderflower, pimento berries, fresh apples and pine needles. The gin has strong African links (unsurprisingly given the name), which come into play. The known botanicals from Africa in this gin include baobab fruit, buchu plant (similar to blackcurrant leaf), African wormwood, lion's tail and devil's claw.

In the context of gin, Elephant Gin has a really unusual line up of botanicals: no orris, no coriander, no angelica and only one citrus (but not the traditional kind) makes for a unique selection that defies expectations of what comes next.

On the nose, there's aromatic dry pine shoots and sweet floral flavours. Other savoury herbal notes emerge in what overall feels like inhaling an earthy forest floor-like gin. To taste, Elephant Gin does not seem like booze stomping around at 45% ABV, as it has an incredibly smooth mouthfeel. Spicy flavours present themselves upfront before the pine and juniper dominate to create a dry, warming gin with a long finish. Combine it with a fan of apple slices in a G&T to bring some light acidity while also complementing the overall gin.

COCKTAILS FOR CLASSIC GINS

There are some cocktails that shine with gins that have more modern flavour profiles, while others are better with a classic, juniper forward gin. No cocktail absolutely requires one or the other so don't let our groupings prevent you from exploring what your favourite gin might be like in any of these cocktails. These are merely our recommendations based on what we feel maximises the potential of each cocktail.

MARTINI

Undoubtedly the most famous of gin cocktails, the Martini is the true test of any bartender's skills. An emblem of style and sophistication; putting the Old Fashioned and Cosmopolitans aside, there are very few other cocktails that can be said to be an icon and to have captivated generations in the way the Martini has. It's also the cocktail that generates the most arguments when trying to decide what constitutes the 'perfect' Martini.

They say that if you are ever lost and alone, start making a Martini, as there will be someone over your shoulder commenting about how you are making it wrong and another to contradict them. However you drink yours, it is good to know how to order your Martini like a pro – no faffing around, no not understanding what you are asking for. It is not only frustrating for the barkeep, but it'll hold you back from exploring the diverse world of this cocktail too.

The transformation of the drink over the past hundred years is intriguing. Its many incarnations are a good reason as to why it can cause such fierce debate, and also good inspiration for finding your perfect serve. We list but nine of the best ones here.

The Original Martini

To begin with the Martini was a different creature entirely, with 1:2 or even 1:1 parts gin and sweet (not dry) vermouth being used, as well as the likely addition of simple syrup or bitters – a sweeter, less bracing beverage. Ingredients like orange bitters remained a relatively frequent ingredient until the 1940s. By the end of the twentieth century, however, the ratio had started to lean more heavily towards the gin until it reached a point where gin was barely caressed with just a touch of vermouth.

With this context in mind, the Martini can be considered more of a broad concept than a specific recipe. The dosage needs to be tailored to the particular gin and vermouth you are using. We feel that the Martini greatly benefits from the big juniper note in classic gins, as it gives you the most options to play around with ratios (mainly because it is more forgiving than when you mix with lighter, more subtle botanicals mixes).

A good rule of thumb, and our favourite, usually goes something like this:

50 ml (2 fl oz) gin
15 ml (½ fl oz) dry vermouth
Citrus zest (matched to the gin)

Pour the gin and dry vermouth into a mixing glass with ice. Stir well, then strain into chilled Martini coupe. Zest the citrus peel and garnish by twisting it in a perfect spiral.

Of course, if you prefer not to use a zest and want an olive, replace the citrus above and garnish appropriately!

Desert Martini or a Churchill Martini
No vermouth is used and the 'Martini' is essentially straight gin diluted with ice and garnished with either a lemon twist or olives. The term 'Churchill' was coined as the former Prime Minister famously used to enjoy his Martinis so dry that he once said, 'I would like to observe the vermouth from across the room while I drink my Martini.'

Bone Dry Martini
Almost no vermouth is used and 'bone dry' is a common way to specify just a whisper of vermouth. In our experience, if you are in a bar ordering an Extra Dry Martini, it amounts to the same thing. Most people make a Bone Dry Martini by rinsing the glass with vermouth and then discarding the excess liquid before pouring in the chilled gin. That way only a trace of the fortified wine is left in the overall mix.

Dry Martini

The lesser the amount of vermouth used, the drier the Martini is considered to be. For most people, when gin is combined with a small amount of dry vermouth, usually in a 6:1 ratio, it is considered dry.

One of our favourite quotes about the Martini directly refers to the Dry Martini. It was popularised in *The Major and the Minor*, a 1942 movie, where Robert Benchley says to Ginger Rogers, 'Why don't you get out of that wet coat and into a Dry Martini?.'

Wet Martini

Gin is combined with a larger amount of dry vermouth, usually in a 3:1 ratio. As with Dry Martinis, a Wet Martini can be ordered 'extra wet' when in a bar, which could go up to as much as 1:1, which, incidentally, is also known as a Fifty-Fifty Martini.

Dirty Martini

This take on the Martini was popularised by President Franklin Roosevelt in the 1930s. Dirty Martinis are generally served with an equal amount of olive brine to vermouth and, given the former is an intense flavour, they are usually made dry. The dirtier the Martini, the more brine one needs to add – so if you are partial to brine in your cocktails, order an 'Extra Dirty' Martini.

Gibson Martini

Gibson Martinis are no longer that common, but by no means should they be condemned to the history books. The Gibson Martini is usually served dry and includes pickled onions instead of olives or citrus as the garnish. It is quite polarising as a drink, but those who like it swear by it.

Vesper Martini

The Vesper Martini was made famous by the 1953 Bond novel and 2006 film *Casino Royale*: 'Three measures of Gordon's, one of vodka, half a measure of Kina Lillet. Shake it very well until it's ice-cold, then add a large thin slice of lemon peel. Got it?.'

Burnt Martini

This little-known variant calls for a splash of Scotch whisky to be added, usually a peaty single malt. We'd suggest avoiding this, and opting for a gin that's been in a peat barrel instead of letting someone lose with the Laphroig, as it's all about the perfect balance, which is incredibly hard to achieve.

NEGRONI

Designed as an aperitif, a good Negroni is the very definition of balance and simplicity. The most widely reported version of this drink's origin is that it was invented at Caffe Casoni in Florence, Italy, in 1919. Legend tells that Count Camillo Negroni asked his friend, bartender Forsco Scarselli, to strengthen his favourite cocktail – the Americano – by replacing the soda water with gin. Scarselli added an orange garnish, rather than the lemon you'd usually get with an Americano, and the drink took off. Before long, everyone was coming into the bar for a 'Negroni'.

Drink it before a good meal, and by good we mean big, because a couple of Negronis would have sunk even Henry VIII. Here we feel like classic gins are the best 'go to' as Campari is such a bold flavour that the gin needs to work hard to counterbalance it, and soft floral numbers or overly citrus forward gins can become a little lost.

20 ml (½ fl oz) gin
20 ml (½ fl oz) sweet vermouth
20 ml (½ fl oz) Campari
Orange peel

Pour the gin, vermouth and Campari into a mixing glass. Add ice and stir until chilled. Strain into a rocks glass and garnish with an orange peel.

NEGRONI BIANCO

If the Negroni is a moustachioed Tom Selleck sitting by a fire, then the Negroni Bianco is Marilyn Monroe in a field of orange blossom, white dress blowing in the wind. It's soft and elegant on the surface, yet an absolute match for its richer and more bitter companion. It's a great alternative to have a trusty recipe for, so if you feel like trying one out, start off here.

30 ml (1 fl oz) gin
20 ml (½ fl oz) Suze
30 ml (1 fl oz) Lillet Blanc
Grapefruit peel

Add all ingredients to an ice-filled glass and stir until cold. Strain into an ice-filled rocks glass and garnish with grapefruit peel.

FRENCH 75

The French 75 is a cocktail held in such high esteem that it falls easily, though with the elegance and grace one would expect of a high-society French Madame, into the realm of the ultimate classic cocktail. It is a drink that suits all styles of gin, but we love it with classic profiles as the juniper note acts as an anchor and grounds the rest of the ensemble with satisfying poise – a firm hold in a classic waltz if you will.

This drink is a tapestry of gin and bubbles, gracefully woven together, and the French 75 is one to turn to in times of celebration – to raise your glass and ring in the new year, the new baby, the new job, the trains being on time . . . yep, that will do.

The cocktail's history goes back further than the 1920s, but one of the first recorded recipes for the French 75 comes from *The Savoy Cocktail Book* (1930). The true nature of its origins is, as often happens with alcohol, slightly muddled. The school of thought that we ascribe to involves Harry MacElhone (owner of Harry's American Bar in Paris). MacElhone never claimed the drink as his own, instead citing McGarry of Buck's Club in London as its conceptual home, and it's unclear who named the drink in 1926.

Nevertheless, the inspiration for the title was apparently a 75mm Howitzer field gun used by the French and the Americans in the First World War. The gun was known for its accuracy and speed, and the French 75 is said to have a kick that it feels like being hit by just such a weapon.

30 ml (1 fl oz) gin
10 ml (2 teaspoons) lemon juice
5 ml (1 teaspoon) sugar syrup
Champagne
Lemon peel

Add the gin, lemon juice and syrup to a cocktail shaker with ice. Shake. Strain into a coupe glass or Champagne flute. Top up with Champagne. Garnish with lemon peel.

RED SNAPPER

The Red Snapper is gin's answer to the Bloody Mary. In our opinion, it works better too – a quick-witted, articulate riposte if you will. It's a tall, refreshing pick-me-up and a drink that was designed with 11am on Sunday in mind.

> 1 pinch of celery salt
> 1 grind of black pepper
> 30 ml (1 fl oz) gin
> 120 ml (4 fl oz) tomato juice
> 15 ml (½ fl oz) lemon juice
> 5 drops of Tabasco pepper sauce
> 3 dashes of Worcestershire sauce
> ½ celery stick

Use the salt and pepper to rim your glass (preferably a Collins). Add the rest of the ingredients – apart from the celery stick – to a cocktail shaker with ice. Shake it. This is the vital part as most build their Bloody Marys in a glass, but with slightly more dilution Red Snappers come to life and slip down that little bit more satisfyingly.

Strain into a glass filled with ice. Add the celery stick to garnish.

RAMOS GIN FIZZ

New Orleans serves as a beacon of light to cocktail fans, home as it is to so many great drinks. While the Hurricane and the Sazerac are great drinks, the Ramos Gin Fizz is, in our opinion, the city's greatest offering.

Originally called The New Orleans Fizz, this cocktail became so popular after its creation in 1888 that it took on the name of its creator – Henry C. Ramos of NOLA's Imperial Cabinet Saloon. Ramos eventually opened up another bar – The Stag – where his drink's reputation really grew, solidifying its place in cocktail history. Legend tells that the Ramos Gin Fizz was so popular that Ramos's bar needed dozens of bartenders working solely on the cocktail. Later, during Mardi Gras in 1915, 35 bartenders were employed. According to Stanley Arthur in *Famous New Orleans Drinks and How to Mix 'Em*, the bar staff 'nearly shook their arms off, and were still unable to keep up with the demand'.

> 60 ml (2 fl oz) gin
> 15 ml (½ fl oz) freshly squeezed lemon juice
> 15 ml (½ fl oz) freshly squeezed lime juice
> 20 ml (½ fl oz) sugar syrup
> 5 ml (1 teaspoon) orange flower water
> 3 drops of vanilla extract
> 1 egg white
> 25 ml (¾ fl oz) double cream
> Sparkling water

Add all the ingredients, bar the sparkling water, to a cocktail shaker and shake hard for a decent amount of time, but without ice. This part is essential (and is called dry shaking) as it helps emulsify the drink and will make it as light as a cloud!

Open the shaker, add ice, seal well and shake again. Strain into a chilled glass and top up with sparkling water.

CONTEMPORARY GINS

Most gins made since 2010 fall into the contemporary category, with the main significant difference between 'modern classic' and 'contemporary' being the extent to which juniper is predominant. There are many gins to try in this category and the three ways to best navigate it are: based on flavour; based on geography; by the maker's spirit.

Flavour

Even in the most complex of recipes, it is always possible to discern certain flavours that shine a little brighter than the rest. This is especially true when you look at them through time and, as we mentioned before, the entire flavour of a gin will not hit you all at once – each botanical has its moment where it's at its most intense. The first flavour zone that you will notice when tasting contemporary gins (as it almost always hits you at the beginning of the journey) is citrus.

Citrus

Bluecoat Gin
One of the first in the new generation of American craft gins, the lemon peel might as well have been zested under your nose as it positively leaps from the glass. While other

notes of juniper and spice on the finish are discernable, it's the instant lift off that marks this gin as unique.

Martin Miller's Gin

With its vivacious lime peel, backed by orange, lemon and the clean nature of cucumber, the gin brings a lively assault on the senses that refreshes and enlivens the palate. The fact that the citrus botanicals are distilled separately from the roots and spices (and the two distillates are then combined before being bottled) will also play a part in the reason they are so bright. Try it with strawberry and cracked black pepper in a G&T as the former complements the front-end excitement, while the latter adds a prolonged depth to the finish.

Ki No Bi Gin

This is a must for those who really want to be transported into a tangy world of exotic citrus. This Japanese gin uses yuzu, a fruit that's deeply evocative of the land in which it is grown, to both begin proceedings and linger on afterwards. Made in Kyoto, Ki No Bi is unusual as, despite the vast scattering of wildcard botanicals, the initial sniff brings a great familiarity with it.

Juniper is clearly present – oily, sappy and rich – but it's the yuzu that quickly makes itself known, filling the nose with a sherbet flush that falls somewhere between mandarin pith and lemon flesh. The other botanicals aren't quiet, but there is also nothing too discernible, save for a flicker of tea. It's an absolute treat of an experience, and one that has set a very high standard for the Japanese craft producers to follow.

Floral

Florals also capture the senses in the world of contemporary gin and tend to be the next most noticeable barrage flavour if they have been used in making the gin. The latest trends are to flavour gin with rose, lavender and elderflower, especially when used in tandem with a flash of citrus.

Pothecary Gin

The simply resplendent use of a bright, zesty lemon peel and an almost overwhelming dose of fragrant lavender in Pothecary Gin creates a unique flavour as heady as the fields of Provence. On the nose, the floral notes really come through – drinkers can close their eyes and be transported to a meadow at first light. Pothecary's clever addition of tilia flowers adds a strong, honey-like smell, while to taste there's a lavender explosion that's both herbal and savoury. These eventually yield to juniper and a marmalade-like lemon peel, the latter circling back to dominate after the tilia flower brings its honeyed sweetness. This is a smooth, full-bodied and bold gin, and certainly worth trying for those with a penchant for a floral taste profile.

Brooklyn Gin

Lavender is used equally brilliantly in Brooklyn Gin – alongside their use of lemon, Persian lime, key lime, sweet orange and kumquat – to create a fantastically fresh gin. We recommend serving it with a grapefruit peel and a sprig of rosemary in a G&T to further enhance the freshness.

Sir Robin of Locksley Gin

The full scope of elderflower, with its soft nose and succulently sweet taste is apparent in Sir Robin of Locksley Gin. It's a profile that's perfectly matched with a grapefruit-flavoured tonic water.

Hendrick's Gin

You would have to have been hiding under a rock not to have seen Hendrick's Gin and, with such consistent messaging, most will have heard about their use of rose and cucumber too. While the G&T 'signature serve' is with a cucumber and most think of it as a big cucumber-flavoured gin, it's really not. In our opinion it is the gin's rosy hues, backed by subtle use of elderflower, chamomile and orange, that are much easier to discern when tasted neat, making it a beautifully floral gin, and one that is deceptively complex too.

Bloom Gin

The best use of floral botanicals to create something intentionally floral without one ingredient overpowering the next is Bloom Gin. The selection of chamomile, pomelo and honeysuckle create a delicate floral balance that's both distinct yet soft. The orangey notes from the pomelo bring a lightness and freshness to the flavour, whilst the honeysuckle provides a rich smoothness, leaving the chamomile to add a gentle floral softness to the gin. The use of juniper, angelica, coriander and cubeb berries underpin the gin. It is this grounding that helps keep it in the style of a London Dry and therein lies Bloom Gin's brilliance. It is not one of those gins that have run away from their heritage. Bloom is surprisingly all too easy to help yourself to very frequently.

Herbal

Herbal flavours, depending on your viewpoint and perception of juniper, could all be considered to be 'classic'. Juniper is decidedly piny and verdant so almost, by definition, herbal. When someone says 'herbal' as a descriptor for gin, however, they tend to either mean savoury (more on this later) or they are talking about rosemary, basil, kaffir lime leaf and, increasingly, Scots pine.

Makar Gin

Made in Glasgow, Makar Gin plays on using a herbal twist with their use of rosemary, which clearly helps to accentuate the verdant nature of their juniper core. One reinforces the other and in the case of Makar, while rosemary isn't evident, the green core to the gin is striking.

Lone Wolf Gin

The carefully calculated use of Scots pine in Lone Wolf Gin, made by Brewdog in Aberdeen, is a masterclass in using the technique of pairing a secondary botanical to accentuate the juniper core, while also allowing it to take over the flavour profile thereafter. First impressions of Lone Wolf are of a strong grapefruit peel aroma mixed with deep, wintery pine, but hold it under your nose for a while and you'll see it's not just juniper, there's also an underlying complexity.

To taste, there is once again the flush of fresh citrus peel upfront, primarily grapefruit, but given some additional bulk by lemon too. The flavours transition fast and the chase is on, driving you straight into the heart of the gin. Before you know it, juniper has stalked you down and is commanding all the attention with its resinous, oily stature. It's quickly followed by Scots pine, which goes in for the killer blow and leaves behind a forest-like finish that refuses to dissipate. One of the great modern gins on the market and easily one of the best gins made in 2017.

Dartmouth Dry Gin

While Twisting Spirits Gin and Bath Gin are other notable entries for their use of kaffir lime leaves, our favourite use of herbs, where rosemary, kaffir lime leaves, Scots pine and a strong backbone of juniper are all in unison, is Dartmouth Dry Gin. Aromatic, fragrant and fresh as an aroma, yet all seemingly balanced in the harmony of the wider gin. There's fresh citrus (grapefruit) and soft florals (rose and lavender), which lead you into the heady green centre of the gin, with an underlying spice (grains of paradise) that pulls you through into a warming finish. It's a great flavour journey, with a booming herbal centre and, overall, a fantastic gin.

Spices

Last but not least in this flavour journey through contemporary gin is spice. Spice is the least explored botanical group by contemporary gin makers, primarily because so many of the botanicals are essentially classic by nature. The most typical are cardamom, cubeb (a cousin of black pepper), cassia and star anise.

East London Liquor Company Gin

Due to its clear juniper, this gin is arguably a 'contemporary classic' and could fit in either category. ELLC, as it's known, is placed here as it uses a truck's worth of cardamom pods to accompany a boisterous juniper, and both can be detected the second the cork is removed. Offset it with a healthy wedge of orange in a G&T.

Bertha's Revenge Milk Gin
Irish made and using a whey base spirit (derived from milk), this is the only other gin that can really go toe to toe with ELLC's cardamom hit. Here the botanical's impression is less fragrant and more curried, akin to the difference between a raw pod and one that's been steamed in pilau rice.

Colonsay Gin
A fine example of the enduring nature that spice can have on the finish of a gin can be found in the Hebredian-made Colonsay Gin. Its use of calamus root (similar to dried ginger) is quite a treat, in particular when accentuated by a green chilli as a garnish in a gin and tonic.

Opihr Gin
The most evidently spiced gin from start to finish is Opihr. On the nose, Opihr Gin has a heady spice mix with cardamom very much raising its hand above the rest of the class. There's also a cheeky, zesty citrus making itself known, adding a light touch to the incoming spice onslaught. While there is certainly an explosion of taste, you are instantly reminded of the vibrant aromas, tastes, noises and colours of exotic spice markets. Cubeb dominates the finish with its deliciously exotic and characterful notes of cracked pepper and light violet. Opihr Gin is an interesting, intoxicating adventure.

Pink Pepper Gin

This is one of our favourite 'spiced' contemporary gins, and is made in the Cognac region of France. There are nine botanicals in Pink Pepper Gin, though only seven are named: juniper, black cardamom, pink peppercorns, cinnamon, honey, vanilla and tonka beans. It is not just the flavour profile that is contemporary either, the distillery makes this gin using vacuum distillation and their still is made entirely from glass. By reducing the atmospheric pressure inside their still (by creating a vacuum), they can distil at lower temperatures, therefore unlocking entirely different sets of flavours.

To the nose, discernable citrus and the pink peppercorns jump to the fore – spicy and arrogantly domineering, but not overly piquant. They lend the tonka bean a helping hand, hefting it up somewhat and pushing it into gourmand, patisserie-like richness. To taste, the gin is gorgeously thick. Complex and curious, the spicy and sweet elements play nicely together. The juniper is slightly herbal and underpins the spirit in a somewhat bossy manner; the sip finishes on a spicy pink-peppered note, but the sweet combination of vanilla, honey and tonka beans are what remain on the tongue long after it's over. The vanilla and tonka beans, incidentally, are infused after distillation, bringing with them an added viscosity and a slight tint to the gin. The mouthfeel is rich and oily and, overall, it is a simply beautiful and entirely bonkers gin.

Geography

Here we raise our glass to the wonderfully transportive nature some gins have. They bring with them a sense of place, take you to a destination and imbue their provenance into every bottle. The idea of travelling through the geography of gin (be it literal or on the impression that they evoke) is a wonderful way to approach the category. In an era where there are thousands of gins at your fingertips, it is a brilliant system to create a selection or an easy criteria to judge what to try next.

Cotswolds Gin

This gin has such a strong sense of geography that one can actually see hedgerows of lavender in a bucolic country setting with each and every taste. It is more than just made there; it also captures the essence of the place. A brilliant distillery and an outstanding flagship gin to keep your eyes on.

Gin Mare

'Herbal' by definition, yes, but this is a full-blown savoury sensation as a gin. It captures the very sun-drenched nature of the Mediterranean basin and has long been the reference point for something that's pushed the boundary of what a gin could taste like.

It smells herbaceous, with resinous juniper and thyme dominating. Once you notice them (they creep up on you) olives are very apparent too. It feels Spanish and triggers memories of tapas, the sweltering sunshine and the feel of the sea all in one. To taste, there's big doses of juniper bursting with basil, rosemary and thyme, which we love serving with a grapefruit peel in a G&T.

St George Terroir Gin

The best example of something truly transportive lies stateside with St George Terroir Gin, which uses three specific botanicals inspired by the Californian wilderness in what the team at St George's Spirits call an 'Ode to the Golden State'. The gin takes its lead from the Douglas fir, bay laurel and sage. Coriander seeds and juniper berries are the other notable botanicals contributing to an aromatic bouquet.

St George Terroir Gin is made using several distillation techniques and then blended together. The team distil the fir and sage individually on a 250 litre (66 US gallon) still to minimise the impact of seasonal variation. Separately, fresh bay laurel leaves and juniper berries are vapour infused in a botanical basket, along with other botanicals, which go in the pot of their 1,500 litre (396 US gallon) still. These three separate distillates are then blended together and cut to the right ABV, at which point the gin is ready for bottling. This fractional, multiple distillate blending approach to distilling was once considered at the frontier of gin innovation, but the method is quite common now in distilleries the world over.

The juniper is slightly subdued, with the defining characteristics being the bay laurel and Douglas fir, which burst out beautifully alongside a lingering, earthy coriander seed spice and warming citrus backdrop. It is, to date, the most memorable, evocative and transformative gin we've had the pleasure to come across.

Isle of Harris Gin

Based on the famous Isle of Harris (land of tweed and azure-like water), the team go as far as diving for sugar kelp to add into their mix, giving the gin a subtle but noticeably sweet and saline quality.

Manly Spirits Gin

Similarly, the Australian gin maker plays on the coastal setting, with clever use of sea lettuce, sea parsley and fresh citrus in their two gins, making them distinct and true to the tag line of capturing nature in a glass. They are both a little sparse on the juniper for some, but it's impossible to deny the deliciously vivid nature of what's been captured.

Ferdinand's Saar Gin

German-made Ferdinand's Saar actually use their vineyard's award-wining Riesling wine to cut their gin to bottling strength, bringing with it the grape's lovely fresh, flinty minerality. As a gin it embodies the literal terroir of a place, as well as the general impression of the region with inimitable effect.

Inverroche Gin

Numerous South African gin makers use their native flora, fynbos, to stunning effect, although they often go a little overboard with the idea at times. Not only is fynbos botanically intense, it varies dramatically all over South Africa, meaning the exact flavour will be different depending on not just which plants are selected, but where the fynbos was harvested. A good contemporary range to try is Inverroche, whose trio of gins reflect this shifting nature as they deliberately forage fynbos from different regions for each of their expressions (and use a hefty dose of it as a botanical during distillation as well as infusing it after).

The Spirit of the Maker

There is a maker's touch that's akin to a painting style for an artist, or the way a particular tone or beat is always audible from certain musicians.

Master distiller Charles Maxwell, a revered seventh generation distiller responsible for some of the best-known gins in the world and the 'go to' contract distiller for hundreds of clients (Maxwell owns and manages Thames Distillery), tends to use winter savoury alongside juniper quite frequently in his stills. On the other hand, former Tanqueray Master distiller and creator of Tanqueray No. Ten, Tom Nichol, has in our opinion a fondness for the textural sweetness provided by liquorice root.

Conniption Gin

There are makers whose entire personalities are reflected in the spirit that they make. For example, Conniption Gin distillers Lee and Melissa Katrincic respect the heritage of gin and learned their craft, but wanted to fuse modern ideas with those time-honoured methods in order to create something new and unique for today. The dual use of copper stills and a rotary evaporator (a glass still that operates at lower atmospheric pressure, similar to that used by Pink Pepper Gin) sets them apart from the rest of the American market. The traditional gin botanicals (juniper, coriander, angelica and cardamom) are placed in the still to be vapour infused, while the more delicate ingredients (honeysuckle and cucumber) are cold distilled in the rotary evaporator, thus preserving their light, fresh tastes and preventing any bitterness from seeping in.

Conniption American Dry has gin heritage instilled in every sip, but the honeysuckle and cucumber ride ahead, bringing with them a modern American, new wave touch to the gin. To taste, cardamom and coriander bring heat, giving the spirit some swagger, while juniper whispers continuously yet quietly in the background with an assuring touch. As a gin, Conniption American Dry does a wonderful job of showcasing the links between science, creativity and personality.

Hernö

This multi award-winning maker is another gin hero in our eyes. Owner and Master distiller Jon Hillegren trained at the Institute of Brewing and Distilling before launching Hernö. Based in the village of Dala, near the city of Härnösand, he began Hernö gin in May 2012 with the ordering of a 250 litre (66 US gallon) German copper pot still called Kierstin.

Hernö Gin uses distinctly Swedish lingonberries and meadowsweet to stunning effect. On the nose, Hernö Gin has a dual note of being piny with a sweet floral backdrop. With hints of citrus and coriander seeds, there is a clear juniper twang complemented by a quietly determined leafy floral note (meadowsweet). The taste is first and foremost led by a lovely freshness, brought on by a pop of lemon and the jammy core of lingonberries, which combine with the meadowsweet to last long after the gin has disappeared. Juniper is carried on too, while more spice comes through towards the end, leading on to a slightly peppery and long finish.

The Scandinavian tones in the London Dry Gin are botanically induced through clever use of local ingredients, but it is in the unfussy modesty – a direct reflection of the temperament of the entire the team there – that its brilliance can be fully appreciated. One of the great gins of all time.

COCKTAILS FOR CONTEMPORARY GINS

Some cocktails, although they may have been invented
long before this Ginaissance, are elevated to the next level
by using contemporary gins and their more progressive
flavour profiles. They may have been designed for classic
gins, but, with some careful consideration, their general
nature and overall impression can be augmented in a
way that's not otherwise possible with juniper forward
gins.

AVIATION

The original recipe for the Aviation cocktail was first
published in Hugo R. Ensslin's 1916 *Recipes for Mixed
Drinks* and made great use of Alps' produced liqueur
crème de violette, the colour of which is alluded to in the
drink's very name.

Harry Craddock later printed the recipe in his 1930
publication, *The Savoy Cocktail Book*. Harry's recipe was a
somewhat corrupt take on the drink as he omitted the
crème de violette – most likely due to its scarcity in Europe
and America (the drink eventually disappeared from the
American market altogether in the 1960s). The absence of
the liqueur meant that for the next forty or so years, the
Aviation was served without one of its central (original)
ingredients. In fact, it wasn't until 2007 that it was brought
back into the American market and even now, cocktail
connoisseurs debate over whether violet has any place in
the drink.

Pick a floral gin to bolster the violette or a citrus
forward gin so that the garnish is better integrated into the
flavour and the mouthfeel on the palate.

50 ml (2 fl oz) gin
10 ml (2 teaspoons) crème de violette
15 ml (½ fl oz) maraschino liqueur
15 ml (½ fl oz) freshly squeezed lemon juice
Cherry or a twist of lemon

Pour the ingredients into an ice-filled cocktail shaker and shake. Strain into a chilled cocktail glass. Garnish with a cherry or a twist of lemon.

CLOVER CLUB

Perfect for contemporary gins, the Clover Club is a pretty-in-pink classic cocktail, with a rich, silky texture and a great complexity that is perfectly balanced to keep most parties happy.

As a drink, the Clover Club predates Prohibition and takes its name from the Philadelphia men's club where it was created. It was something of an old boys' club, established by lawyers and bankers in the Bellevue-Stratford Hotel in the 1880s. It is unknown when and by whom the drink was originally made, but by 1910 it was being sold far outside the city of Philadelphia, in hotels like The Plaza in New York City.

It's obvious to see how a fruity gin might double down on the grenadine, but our advice is to pick a contemporary profile that has plenty of soft citrus (like apricots or warm oranges) or soft florals (like elderflower) to complement the nature of the cocktail as opposed to accentuating just one area.

50 ml (2 fl oz) gin
10 ml (2 teaspoons) lemon juice
5 ml (1 teaspoon) grenadine (or raspberry syrup)

10 ml (2 teaspoons) sweet vermouth
Handful of fresh raspberries, plus 1 to garnish
1 egg white

'Dry shake' all the ingredients in a cocktail shaker for about 30 seconds until the egg has emulsified and the berries have been pulverised. Then add half a cup of ice, then shake again until cold and fine strain into a chilled coupe glass and garnish with a raspberry.

BRAMBLE

The Bramble is a blackberry-based cocktail that's as simple to make as it is nicely balanced in its sweet-and-sour tones. It works well with all types of flavour styles, but for a delicious twist, pick something that has a warming spiced tone to it and it'll bring in a much earthier feel to the cocktail.

The Bramble is the brainchild of Dick Bradsell, aka 'The Cocktail King'. The blackberry drink is arguably the most famous of his creations from his time at Fred's Club Soho in the 1980s, and is often compared to that of Jerry Thomas' Gin Fix, swapping the latter's raspberry syrup for blackberry liqueur. The drink is said to take its name from the winding nature that the liqueur takes when it's poured from the top to the bottom of the glass, as though it were dodging through brambles.

The cocktail is on its way to modern classic status, if it hasn't already reached it, frequenting more bars than Ernest Hemingway and Oliver Reed combined.

50 ml (2 fl oz) gin
25 ml (¾ fl oz) freshly squeezed lemon juice

10 ml (2 teaspoons) sugar syrup
15 ml (½ fl oz) crème de mûre
Freshly picked blackberries or crème de framboise

Add the gin, lemon and sugar syrup to a cocktail shaker.
Shake well. Strain into an ice-filled rocks glass. Trickle the
crème de mûre over the top, creating the 'bramble' type
effect.

Garnish with freshly picked blackberries or, for a fruity
summer twist, add a splash of crème de framboise.

BASIL SMASH

The Basil Smash is a relatively new drink (well, new in the
context of well-known cocktails) with an alluring green tint
and a fresh kick. In fact, the addition of fresh basil means
that this drink is basically a vegetable, and certainly a
welcome way to get one of your five-a-day . . .

Pick a herbal gin if you want to further the verdant
tones of this cocktail, but our favourite contrast is to pick a
contemporary gin with a big flush of florals because doing
so creates a sense of the garden in a glass.

*1 bunch of basil leaves (if in doubt as to how much, go
    heavy on the basil)*
25 ml (¾ fl oz) freshly squeezed lemon juice
15 ml (½ fl oz) sugar syrup
50 ml (2 fl oz) gin

Place the basil and lemon into a cocktail shaker. Gently
muddle the lemon and basil, 'smashing' the ingredients.
Add the sugar syrup and gin and top up with ice. Shake

vigorously. Double strain into an ice-filled rocks
glass. Garnish with basil leaves.

OLD TOM GINS

As a sub-category, Old Tom Gin is often misunderstood as
simply the spirit that started the gin craze. It wasn't. It
arrived as a style towards the end of the eighteenth century,
not the beginning. However, Old Tom Gin is a perfect
starter spirit for those new to the category. Its sweetness
makes it more accessible than London Dry Gins, and the
botanical intensity delivers huge flavours, helping to stir
the imagination and give drinkers a clear picture of what
it is they're tasting. Old Tom Gin bottles usually nod
to tradition, and depict a cat (usually black) somewhere
on them.

From the 1800s onwards, Old Tom was the
preeminent style of respectable gin, with the likes of
Tanqueray, Beefeater and Gordon's offering their own
versions of Old Tom. Tanqueray recently brought
theirs back in a limited edition run, recreating the
original recipe.

As a style, Old Tom's fall from grace was slow and
gentle as drinkers moved towards drier gins over a period
of a century, brought on by the advent of new distilling
technology and advances made by engineers such as Anneas
Coffey in 1830. These improvements were primarily to the
distillation of the base spirit (Coffey patented the two-
column continuous still, which produced a spirit with a
higher proof and lighter character).

Due to the base spirit being lighter in flavour or in
essence, it became more neutral, so there was simply less
of a need to 'mask' it with sweeteners such as sugar. With

less sugar being used, just as in wine, the term used to describe the flavour of gin became 'Dry' and thus, a new style was born.

Fast forward even further and by 2005, Old Tom Gin was so scarce in its availability that there were less than a dozen brands offering an Old Tom variety across the world. Thankfully, the global hunger for classic cocktails in the noughties (see page 9) meant that Old Tom enjoyed a resurgence of its own.

The first British brand to reinvigorate the genre was Hayman's Old Tom in 2007, whilst in the US it was Ransom Old Tom a few years later.

The Naming of Old Tom

As with the majority of gin's history, the term Old Tom Gin itself is shrouded in mystery and mistruths. The story we tend to favour is that of Tom Chamberlain, who was a distiller at the Benjamin Hodges Distillery in the 1800s. Not just because we think it is the most likely, but because it is so closely tied to how gin was made, sold and consumed in the early 1800s.

In the years that followed the Gin Craze (1720–1750), gin making was rare. By the 1800s, raw spirit was being made in large volume distilleries who then sold it on to smaller rectifiers who, for the sake of simplification here, were more akin to flavourists than distillers. Spirits were subject to heavy government taxes and regulations and although a few respectable firms had been established, hard liquor, and gin in particular, had not yet overcome the stigma of its association with one of the darkest times of London's history.

The spirit being made hadn't really improved in quality either, as most distilleries were operations where the focus was on scale and scale alone. Alcohol was made from a range of base ingredients, including spoiled wheat, cereals and, quite commonly, oats. In an age where famine was a constant threat, using good crops to make alcohol instead of food was obscene. This wasn't the preserve of the British, rather the prevailing attitude around the world at the time, as demonstrated by the archives on display in the two dedicated Genever Liqueur museums, Nationaal Jenevermuseum in Schiedam, Netherlands, and Jenevermuseum in Hasselt, Belgium.

Despite it's pokey nature, this raw spirit was sold to a rectifier, or directly to a compounder/retailer who would add a mix of botanicals to flavour it (juniper to make gin, but sometimes fruits and spices for other products), then use water to cut it to retail strength. To mask the poor spirit, as well as juniper, distillers added in larger quantities of strong, sweet botanicals such as liquorice root, creating a sweeter style of spirit, as well as pungent spices to mask the less than smooth finish.

By the mid-nineteenth century, gin had begun its rise from the depths of depravity, though it was still seen as the drink of the lower classes. This meant that while widely served, it was not really valued. Cheap and poorly made gins were very much the *only* gins being consumed at this time. It was in this world that old Tom Chamberlain's gins, shortened to 'Old Tom's Gin', became the byword for the best quality gin made in the sweet style of the time. Soon, it wasn't just Chamberlain's gin that carried the name, but everyone who made gin, desperate to muster some of the respectability it had started to command.

Old Tom Gins were sweetened with sugar beet, cane sugar, partially refined sugar (such as muscovado), highly refined sugar, honey and other naturally sweet botanicals, like chamomile or liquorice. Brands of Old Tom today use a variety of sweeteners, often derived from various sources, with modern influences even starting to emerge with stevia being added in the likes of Californian-made Anchor Old Tom Gin.

Ageing (or not) plays a key role in Old Tom Gin debates and no one is quite sure what constitutes the more historically accurate. In our opinion, it is likely both ideas are true and, regardless, both can be enjoyed today.

Ransom Old Tom Gin

This US brand is deliberately aged in oak barrels. For the brand, this time in oak adds both to the flavour and to the historical accuracy of their gin, as even though gin may not have been intentionally aged by makers in the 1800s, it would have been transported in casks thereafter and, from a US perspective, that would have meant months, not weeks before it arrived at the destination, so the prolonged time spent in cask must have had a significant impact on the flavour. It's not the sweetness, nor the oak, that really marks Ransom Old Tom though, but the grainy undertones and cereal-like note that permeate throughout.

Portobello Old Tom Gin

A limited edition gin, Portobello Old Tom Gin was both sold by the bottle as a 'lightly rested spirit' and kept above The Distillery bar in an old sherry barrel (as a nod to the Old Tom barrels depicted in the famous Cruickshank illustrations of the gin palaces of old) to allow it to evolve over time. This allowed for a fascinating glimpse into what it might have been like in the Dickensian era, where spirits were constantly – intentionally or not – evolving.

Hayman's Old Tom Gin

This is what many British bartenders will be familiar with. As one of the key brands to bring back the genre and popularise it once more, Hayman's has become a reference point. It's very similar in flavour to their flagship dry gin, but the orange peel is more pronounced with its lovely caramelised warmth and the liquorice root is notably increased for that definitive sweetness that lingers on the finish. It is not aged as the Hayman's family felt that most British-made Old Toms would have been transported in casks for too short a period of time to really impact the flavour of the gin, and that the interaction would not have been much anyway, given the barrels would have been re-used many times so they were what we would now call inert.

Hernö Old Tom Gin

Similarly not ageing theirs, Hernö uses organic, local honey, making use of Sweden's largest honey farm only 5 km (3 miles) away from the distillery. They have also accentuated the dose of meadowsweet they add as a botanical, giving the gin a heady top note that is simply sublime.

Citadelle No Mistake Old Tom Gin

This is a good example of all of the elements that make up this genre of gin – sweetened, aged, a cat on the label and a delicious elixir to taste! While hard to get hold of, it was in our top five best gins of 2017 as it is a superb example of the heights that can be achieved with this style of gin but also, irrespective of any context, it's simply an extraordinary mélange of flavours.

On the nose, there's lashings of juniper, orange zest and cardamom all evident, but with a softer floral touch of jasmine and honeysuckle floating just above. To taste, the barrel-ageing process and use of sugar are clear – sweetness flushes through with deeper fruit cake-like sensations, leaving behind a deliciously long, woody sensation.

COCKTAILS FOR OLD TOM GINS

Sweet in nature and usually rich with boisterous flavours, Old Tom Gins have a very unique place in the cocktail cabinet. Not only are they a brilliant choice for cocktails where you'd like to add in a touch of sweetness without resorting to sugar syrup, they are also handy for those who want to try and accurately recreate old recipes from the turn of the twentieth century, which often call for Old Toms. Here are two such recipes, which both suit the genre's flavours. They are from the turn of the century and make for delicious history in a glass.

MARTINEZ

This is an elegant post-dinner cocktail, perfect for Old Tom Gins, but carries enough spirit to see you through a night of debauchery. An added bonus is how much you can upsell your sophistication levels by ordering this drink . . . Just don't get smug about it – you should have been calling for these for a long time now.

50 ml (2 fl oz) Old Tom Gin
20 ml (½ fl oz) sweet vermouth
10 ml (2 teaspoons) dry vermouth
5 ml (1 teaspoon) marachino liqueur

1 dash of Boker's Bitters
Orange twist

Add all of the ingredients to a cocktail shaker filled halfway
with ice. Stir. Strain into a chilled Martini glass. Garnish with
an orange twist.

TOM COLLINS

One of the first recorded Tom Collins recipes is from the
second edition of Jerry Thomas' book, *The Bartender's
Guide*, published in 1876, in which Tom Collins is a class
of drink, with the type of alcoholic spirit being used
specified after the name Tom Collins (e.g. '-brandy', '-gin').
It was others who came after Thomas – 'the father of
American mixology' – who changed the Tom Collins
from its three main variations into a purely gin drink.

The name derives from a hoax in New York in 1874:
Tom Collins was a fictitious man rumoured to sit in taverns
and loudly bad-mouth people. 'Good' friends of those he
was overheard insulting would encourage the injured party
to find Tom Collins and confront him. Those seeking him
would ask at the bar for Tom Collins and receive this sour
cocktail instead of a black eye. Despite being named after a
hoax, the Tom Collins has been immortalised as one of the
most iconic gin cocktails around.

50 ml (2 fl oz) Old Tom Gin
25 ml (¾ fl oz) freshly squeezed lemon juice
15 ml (½ fl oz) sugar syrup
Soda
Orange slice

Combine the first three ingredients in a Collins glass with ice.
Stir and then top up with soda. Garnish with an orange
slice.

NAVY STRENGTH GINS

As recently as 2012, higher proof 'navy' offerings were only
made by a handful of brands. Because of this, so much of
what is known about Navy Strength Gin today is the result
of a tangled combination of historical fact and marketing
myths (mainly from Plymouth Gin). Thankfully, since their
revival Navy Strength Gins have exploded in popularity
once more.

While records are hard to find (it is far easier to track
rum rations given to sailors), there is a lot of peripheral
evidence to suggest that the British Navy was an important
buyer and a valued client for numerous gin distilleries over
the centuries. According to the Plymouth Gin archives, at
the height of the East India Trading Company in the early
1800s, the Navy allegedly consumed thousands of barrels
a year.

As we know, the quality of gin produced around the
UK varied and it was often suspected that the spirit had
been overly watered down. To test the strength (thus the
perceived quality) of the alcohol, it is reputed that the Navy
mixed gunpowder with gin, placed it in a special contraption
and lit it. If it burned with a clear flame, this was 'proof'
that the spirit was of sufficient strength. Failure to light or a
smoky flame were signs that the spirit was below the
required strength and would be rejected. To pass this test,
when creating gins for the Navy, distillers supplied it at a
strength of 57% ABV or higher.

Another story goes that the Navy needed its spirits to be above a certain ABV so that in the event that they were spilled during battle, gunpowder would still light. This is highly unlikely to be true as spirits would be rationed and given out at specific times and under strict control, while ammunition stores were at the heart of most ships, quite far away from where the booze would lie. No captain would send instructions for a booze 'top up' in the midst of battle, so if one was sloshing around in the company of the other, the boat would either be already sinking or it would be because there was a mutinous crew . . .

It was only really in modern times (and from our research it seems during a very specific marketing campaign for Plymouth Gin in the late nineties) that this higher alcoholic level was given the moniker 'Navy Strength'.

Historically, records suggest that Navy Strength Gins would have tasted earthier and rootier than what we know today, due to their use of botanicals such as angelica, liquorice and coriander, and spices like cinnamon and lemongrass, as well as the base spirit not being as clean and neutral as what is used in modern times. This modern myth, though, seems to have been misunderstood as meaning higher proof gins do not include citrus. This is not true and there is no clear evidence to suggest that Navy Strength did not include peels. We know that even at this time it was certainly possible, as Lucas Bols, which supplied the Dutch East India Company with many fruit cordials and liqueurs such as curacao, demonstrated.

These days, Navy Strength Gin doesn't have a 'signature' botanical flavour profile in the way that Old Toms are defined by sweetness (often liquorice) or classic gins by the forward nature of juniper and coriander seeds.

Citrus, herbal, spiced or fruity – all are possible to find in the Navy sub-category. The only thing that unifies the entire genre is its high alcohol content of 57% ABV.

Plymouth Navy Strength Gin

The Plymouth Gin Distillery (formerly known as the Black Friars Distillery and once a Dominican monastery built in 1431) is central to the Navy Strength genre. Their bottling is by far the most iconic and the best-known higher-proof gin offering in the world.

Plymouth Navy Strength Gin is more aggressively charged than its 'Original' strength sister, with the spirit flicking at your nostrils and letting you know that it's high proof booze in your glass. The juniper is more assertive, the spice notes of cardamom are more pronounced and the lemon peel notes seem brighter. Higher proof gins, in general, favour more spiced botanicals, and while this is true, the gin has more than a good volley of citrus to enliven the palate!

Scapegrace Navy Strength Gold Gin

From New Zealand, this gin illustrates how it is possible to achieve brilliant citrus, as well as maintain a big mouthfeel, at a higher proof. The key to its success is the addition of tangerine peels. There's huge spice and a lashing of booze, but it's joined by fleshy, juicy citrus fruits that surround the experience in a cacophony of intense zesty flavours.

Perry's Tot Navy Strength Gin

For fans of Plymouth Gin looking for an alternative that shares many of the same cues, this Brooklyn, New York, gin was one of the first American Navy Gins and a treat to discover. Most of the botanicals used are relatively traditional (juniper, cinnamon, cardamom, star anise and citrus peels) but there is one unusual botanical: wild flower honey from upstate New York, which adds both texture and a subtle backdrop.

The label is printed on the inside with an illustration of Lord Perry, a wink to Plymouth's infamous monk, which adorns the inner cover of historic bottles. A wink perfectly describes what the gin is about too – a modern interpretation of a classic style and a lovely riff off Plymouth Gin. It's juniper forward, though surrounded on all sides by warming spices and an orange hue. Once the tongue is used to the spirit sensation, grapefruit and lingering flavours of star anise and cinnamon emerge.

Campfire Navy Strength Gin

Made by Puddingstone Distillery in the Chilterns, England, the botanicals at hand in Campfire Navy Strength Gin (and, indeed, Campfire Gin) are juniper, orris, coriander, angelica, roasted hazelnut, physalis, orange peel, grapefruit peel and rooibos. The nose is full of warm pine and rich, festive oranges, and to taste, it's perfumed and oily, with oranges coating the tongue in a thick, sweet syrup and fiery coriander doing double time with the high ABV.

Juniper pushes its way through, thick and sappy, like the resin you get when you squish berries between your finger and thumb. The back of the sip is dominated by the hazelnuts, which bring a rich, sweet quality that sits pretty on the tongue, watching the other botanicals waltz by. Sip it neat – you'll be amazed.

Tarquin's Seadog Navy Strength Gin

Created in Cornwall and another firm favourite of ours, the idea for 'Seadog' as it's affectionately known began as a run of 771 bottles of Navy Strength, which were created to mark the disbanding of the 771 Naval Air Squadron in 2016. Having proved incredibly popular, the Southwestern Distillery team decided to re-launch it later that year as a permanent member of the gin range.

The recipe's ingredients are the same as that of the distillery's much-loved flagship Tarquin's Dry Gin, though the botanicals, in particular juniper, have been ramped up ever so slightly. To nose, a vivid and fresh resinous juniper crashes the senses. This bracing directness allows for an underlying cinnamon fire and warm coriander seed citrus to sneak up behind and, before you know it, you've been swept away in the moment.

To taste, Tarquin's Seadog Navy Strength Gin is possibly one of the best gins of all time. It grabs your juniper-loving soul and embraces it with a generous lashing of pine and citrus. It is made in tiny batches by a team that is both charming and easygoing, transparent with what they do, collaborative in their philosophies and progressive in their attitudes as to what it is possible to make.

COCKTAILS FOR NAVY STRENGTH GINS

With their higher ABV, Navy Strength Gins can pack a punch in any cocktail. Replace your usual gin with a Navy Strength Gin and just see the difference! The following are two cocktails that are not just at their best with higher proof gins, but were specifically invented using them. Each has a clear maritime history and each really needs that extra vigour that only higher proof offerings can bring to really shine. This unique combination of fantastic taste and historical context makes for a couple of recipes you'll want to get familiar with . . .

THE GIMLET

The Gimlet is a light green, lime-heavy cocktail with a rich naval history and a sharp kick.

The Gimlet was first promoted and drunk by British officers back in the nineteenth century. Citrus juice was a gift from the gods to sailors as it prevented them from getting scurvy – a brutal, painful and sometimes deadly disease brought about by vitamin C deficiency.

Rear-Admiral Sir Thomas Desmond Gimlette (served 1879–1913) is cited by some as the namesake of the Gimlet. Acting as a doctor in the Navy, he administered lime with gin in order to mask the bitter taste. Apparently, he introduced this to his shipmates to help them swallow down the lime juice as an anti-scurvy medication. British sailors, though – unlike their officer superiors – had rum rations, and so used to mix this in with their lime. The drink became known as 'grog' and so great was their consumption of this 'medicine' that sailors soon became known as 'limeys'.

50 ml (2 fl oz) Navy Strength Gin
10 ml (2 teaspoons) Rose's lime juice cordial

Add both ingredients to a mixing glass with ice. Stir. Strain into a chilled Martini glass.

The Pink Gin

Pink Gin is a Royal Navy cocktail classic with a history dating back to the 1800s. The drink is sharp and heavy, with its alluring colour hinting at its rich, dry taste (and its somewhat dizzying effects). This is a cocktail very well suited to the end of a long day. It's no fuss to fix up and it'll leave you with a nice, leisurely buzz.

> *3 dashes of Angostura bitters*
> *50 ml (2 fl oz) Navy Strength Gin*
> *Lemon zest*

There are two ways to make this drink – one involves rolling the bitters around the glass to coat, then tipping out the excess and pouring in ice-cold gin from the freezer. The other involves combining both ingredients and stirring with ice, then straining it into a chilled coupe glass. We opt for the latter. Garnish with lemon zest.

Barrel-aged Gin

There are many gins that are intentionally barrel-aged, and the 'aged' genre is one of the fastest growing sectors of the gin industry.

Bourbon Barrel'ed, Barrel Rested, Cask Aged, Oak Aged, Matured or even 'Yellow' Gin – there are many names attributed to gins that have been mellowed in casks. The term on the tag might be versatile, but the process remains the same as it always has – lay the gin to rest and let the alchemy of time do its magic.

The important aspects to note for those trying to understand the genre are the type of wood and the size of the cask being used, the previous occupant of the cask (what was formerly being aged in there, if anything) and the overall maturation time. All four impact the spirit greatly.

Whisk(e)y and Cognac fans will tell you that no matter what may or may not have been in a barrel before, the oak itself will impart its own distinct identity. The type of oak used in a 'virgin barrels', as they are known when they are fresh out of the cooperage, has a character of its own due to the way the trees grow and the climate they lived in.

American oak is richer in its sugary sweetness, French oak has soft, almost nutty tannins, while casks made from sappy juniper wood (which are very rare) add a resinous smell so potent it can be akin to a bouquet of freshly shorn pencils. When used to make a cask, each wood type imparts a tone to any spirit that the vessel contains.

The size of the cask makes an impact on the surface area interacting with the spirit. The smaller the cask, the larger the ratio is and the faster the interaction occurs. For rapid maturation, ginsmiths use small barrels, while for longer-term maturation they use larger vessels.

It is fair to say that the previous occupant of a barrel will leave the most obvious trace to taste. Despite the previous liquid being removed before gin goes in, the casks will have absorbed several litres of liquid into the oak itself and the casks are deliberately kept 'wet' to preserve the integrity of the vessel (as barrels dry out, they shrink a little and loosen up, meaning they can become leaky).

This residue will leach out into the subsequent spirit: ex-bourbon barrels will add distinct notes of charred vanilla; beautiful tropical fruit notes will come through when using rum casks and casks that previously held sherry will impart the dried fruit tones of sultanas and raisins. If the previous contents was peated whisk(e)y, you can expect smoke to have impregnated the wood and the gin; if a barrel previously held Chardonnay or Sauvignon Blanc, it will influence the gin flavour too.

A fun way to explore these differences is to look at the Pickering's Gin barrel-aged range, in which they place the same gin into various barrels from around Scotland. It is possible to see how the regional styles of the nation's famous Scotch distillers impact the gin's profile as each tastes so different to the next, and makes for a brilliant range to taste side by side.

Once the type of wood, the size of the cask and what it previously contained have all been selected, gin makers have to decide how long they should leave their gin in. Too long and the oak overwhelms the gin, turning the flavour from botanically gorgeous to akin to sucking on the end of a twig. Too little and it will be too sympathetic to the original gin and not have altered it enough. Typically, however, most Barrel-aged Gins lie dormant for three to nine months.

Within a few weeks a barrel will influence the gin it contains into becoming something else. Sometimes, a long conversation is needed to subdue and alter the botanicals; other times a few short moments will suffice to dramatically affect the way a gin presents itself and behaves in your glass.

9 Moons and 26 Moons

Martin Miller's two limited edition barrel-aged releases reflect the alchemy of time, and demonstrate the different pace that some barrels take to reach the perfect harmony. The two gins are aged in two different barrels: 9 Moons was rested in an American oak barrel that previously contained bourbon for nine months; 26 Moons was aged in French oak that previously contained Madeira wine. It took the ex-Madeira cask a year and a half longer to take on the desired character and reach a perfect balance of underlying spirit than the 9 Moons, hence their names. The two gins are very different, yet both showcase 'aged gin' beautifully, while delivering a tasty spirit that's a delight to sip on.

The Cask at the Back

For those who like a fun anecdote at the bar, the longest maturation in modern times that we have come across is this gin, from Fifty Pounds Gin. 'Cask at the Back' refers to barrels that are stored at the back of the warehouse and are usually there for longer than those at the front (since access was more difficult before the era of forklifts and palletised racking). In this case, the gin spent seven years in a barrel that previously held PX Sherry. An excessive maturation no doubt, but we can confirm that it is delicious.

Burrough's Reserve Gin

Beefeater Distillery's barrel-aged offering is one of the few cask-aged gins that are available around the world. Distilled using James Burrough's original copper 'Still Number 12', the gin is then rested in red and white Bordeaux oak casks with a capacity of only 268 litres (71 US gallons) each. These carefully selected casks imbue the gin with their subtle characteristics of both the oak and residual Bordeaux wines, giving the bottled spirit a soft, oaked spice aroma. Richer, juniper-led spice develops to taste along with a hint of dried fruit on the finish.

Garden Swift Aged Gin

Made in Oxfordshire by an unassuming team intent on the quiet pursuit of fantastic flavours and perfectly ripe fruit, the yearly release of Garden Swift (formerly Garden Tiger) Aged Gin is a must try for spirits connoisseurs. Placed in a mulberry barrel, fresh from ageing a Harry Masters Jersey Apple Eau de Vie, the gin is left to mature. The apple Eau de Vie adds a sweet interplay of orchard fruits to the underlying juniper forward and orange zest-laced gin. Meanwhile, the mulberry wood itself adds an unusual combination of spice and floral notes, and a simply stunning toffee colour to the spirit. The releases changes each year as the product is a 'vintage', but to date, all have been incredible releases . . .

Across the world, almost every gin maker will have dabbled in the dark art of maturing their gins. Many confuse boldness with balance though, and while they produce loud flavours and hugely oaked flavours, few have actually benefited from the sweet slumber of time in a cask.

Internationally, the aged gins to note (in which the gin has been elevated to a new level) are the aforementioned Peat Barreled Big Gin from Seattle; Hernö's Juniper Cask Gin with it's sappy demeanour; Tasmania-based Süd Polaire and their Rare Oak Cask gin, which brings layers of toasted nougat to the mouthfeel, and lastly Chicago-based FEW Spirits and their Barrel Gin, which brings a heavy dose of sweetness that's irresistible in a cocktail.

A COCKTAIL FOR BARREL-AGED GINS

Neat over ice is how many serve their Barrel-aged Gins, mainly as most are not at their best in a G&T. The cask tends to clash with tonic (there are exceptions to this rule), so if you are looking at long, refreshing serves, look towards ginger ale or ginger beer, or even soda water, as you might with a Scotch whisk(e)y highball. We feel that to really savour all the complexity of an aged gin, however, Old Fashioneds are where you need to head . . .

GIN OLD FASHIONED

There's none so simple, yet so complex, as the Old Fashioned, a cocktail so historic that it earned its moniker in or around 1880. The gin equivalent of this drink is a funny old thing; dry as a bone, despite its sugary make-up, and deliciously rich. We think it is probably the way to drink Barrel-aged Gin; in fact, there are some that work so well in this combination that it almost feels like destiny. As a cocktail it's smooth, sultry and effortlessly dignified, perfect for dim lights and late nights.

1 lump of sugar (preferably demerara)
2–3 dashes of Angostura bitters
40 ml (1½ fl oz) Barrel-aged Gin
Orange peel

Drop the sugar lump into the bottom of a rocks glass and splash the bitters over it. Muddle the two together until you've formed something of a paste. A dash – the smallest dash – of water will help quicken this process along.

Add about half of the gin to the glass, then stir until the sugar has dissolved. Fill the glass with ice, then top up with the rest of the gin. Give it a quick final whirl and add the orange peel.

FRUIT GINS AND INFUSIONS

Fruit-infused gin seems like a booming trend that's so 'millennial' in its pink-tastic Instagrammable nature that it is easy to assume it is a new or even a modern thing.

In Britain, it is quite the opposite. Sloe gin, for example, along with a lot of other infused gins, comes from the eighteenth century when the Enclosure Acts (a series of Acts of Parliament that enabled landowners to enclose open fields and common land in England and Wales) led to hedgerows popping up all over the country. The hedgerow fruit that grew on these blackthorn bushes flavoured and masked the terrible gin of the time, along with sweeteners including sugar.

SLOE GIN

Sloe gin has its own designated status and is the only type of fruit infusion that is allowed to be have the name gin on it, yet be under the 37.5% ABV. All other fruit infusions have to be termed as liqueurs, or be over the required alcohol level – meaning that something like the damson gins (typically bottled around 26% ABV) are technically illegal, but who's really looking . . .

To make a sloe gin at home, pick a good, classically styled juniper forward gin. Plump for something that's got a decent strength too, as the sloes will reduce the ABV during the process, soaking some up as it goes along. When the time is right, pick sloe berries and, once washed, place them in the gin, seal it and leave it be for a few weeks.

Contrary to popular belief, there is very little point in adding sugar at the outset as saturating the spirit with sugar prevents it from extracting the natural fruit sugars – and other flavours – from the sloes. Moreover, one of the common complaints about most sloe recipes is that some years they produce a too-sweet liqueur, while other years are not sweet enough. Sweetening to taste at the end of the maceration yields a perfect batch every time, and so while it's handy to have a recipe, the best results are always achieved by those doing it after, and doing it to taste.

A top tip for those who are feeling adventurous: if you like the marzipan flavours in sloe gins, understand that this is because of the stone at the centre. Crushing a few (not all) of the sloes before you macerate them in gin will increase this flavour as there is more direct interaction with the stone. Alternatively, add a couple of almonds into the mix, which will complement the marzipan note, and make significantly less mess . . .

In the UK, the countryside and fruit-infused gins are so firmly intertwined that sloe, damson, bullace and quince infusions are sometimes called 'Hunting Gins' as a micro category, as they are often the tipples decanted into hip flasks for countryside pursuits.

OTHER FRUIT GINS

Hedgerow fruits aside, in the forgotten history of gin's unglamorous years through the 1960s to 1980s, orange and lemon gin infusions were mainstream global releases. Plymouth Orange Gin is the most notable vintage expression from this era. Gordon's also had a mint infusion at the start of the 1900s, as well as one with ginger. Some of these historic recipes are being brought back today (Tanqueray Flor de Sevilla for example), although the trend is decidedly more berried-pink than citrus hued for now.

Puerto de Indias is a well-known Spanish strawberry-infused gin launched circa 2015. The romanticism conjured by the name is probably the nicest thing to say about the pink liquid, which is extremely sweet and more bubble-gum flavoured than natural. In 2018, Beefeater and Gordon's released their own strawberry gin editions with huge commercial success and, in our opinion, a better gauge on how best to dose the flavours of juniper and strawberry together. In a G&T, double down on the pink with the garnish and opt for more strawberries or raspberries.

Another early adopter (2015) of all things pink is Pinkster Gin. They use the fruit in the botanical mix during distillation as well as infuse more in after. Fresh and bright, yet surprisingly verdant and botanically broad, while it looks like a pretty in pink number, the flavours are much more developed. And, with no added sugar or sweetener, the dry finish and real fruit shine through. Serve it with a bravely sized mint sprig in a G&T.

Pimm's is still one of the most popular gin-based fruit liqueurs for British summertime, of course, although most would be very hard pressed if asked to discern the underlying gin. Elderflower-infused gins tend to be bottled commercially as liqueurs as opposed to high proof gins, with good examples to seek out being Edinburgh Gin's Elderflower Liqueur and the Lakes Distillery Elderflower Gin Liqueur — both of which are bright with candied floral notes. Try them with soda or lemonade in a pitcher, along with some citrus wheels to garnish.

The major trend for 'pink' in the UK has been rhubarb, and if this tickles tastebuds just reading the words 'rhubarb' and 'gin' strung in the same sentence, then we particularly recommend Warner Edwards Victoria's Rhubarb Gin.

Distilled by former farmers, the flavour of this gin tasted neat is excellent, with a pleasing acidity and delightfully light (given it's still a 40% ABV gin). There are hints of lemon with an earthy sweetness. Unsurprisingly, the rhubarb is BIG and tangy, but not at the expense of the underlying gin, which can be uncovered if you take a little time to taste the spirit. It is that base gin that plays a large part in balancing out the overall flavour. We love adding it to ginger ale instead of tonic as the sweet sour nature of the gin works beautifully off the piquant nature of the other.

Other brands to look out for include Australian Four Pillars Bloody Shiraz Gin. To make the infusion, Shiraz grapes are harvested when they are sweet and ripe, de-stemmed and then soaked in the distillery's Rare Dry Gin for around eight weeks, gently stirred every day. Their colour, flavour and sweetness slowly bleeds out into the gin in a slightly different way with each bottling, depending on the grape harvest that year. The 2017 vintage was a little less sweet than the 2016, but still coated the tongue with a superbly candied, stewed-fruit taste. The richness of the fruit is even more apparent in the 2018 edition, and while the finish keeps true to the Rare Dry Gin spice, the Shiraz grapes gave the gin's caramelised orange notes extra vigour that lingers on.

While not fruit infusions, a popular trend, and proving that 'ginfusions' are a riot of colour, is using pea flower. The iridescent flower tints the gin ink blue. Six Dogs Karoo

(South Africa) have a blue version, while Empress 1908 is a Canadian gin that infuses the flower afterwards, but the one we have a soft spot for is Portuguese made Sharish. The aroma of bright citrus comes from the distillery's use of apples, as well as orange peel, lemon peel and lemon verbena – all of which are in stark contrast to the deep blue liquid in front of your eyes. To taste, there is more earthiness to the ensemble, but the overall impression is that of a light, accessible gin. The fun part? The liquid changes with alterations in pH level (i.e. with the addition of acid or alkaline), so when you add tonic, it goes from blue to pink.

For those who prefer a more straightforward synaesthetic association and for pink to signify floral, a top trending product in South Africa is the rose water-infused Musgrave Pink Gin. The spirit has a distinctly perfumed flavour (due to the rose water, but also the use of rosehip as a botanical) and one that blooms in a glass. Try it with soda water instead of tonic for maximum effect.

HOME INFUSIONS

Infusing gin using your own botanicals or fruit can be incredibly fun and make for brilliant twists on classic cocktails. Don't limit yourself to just fruit – one of our favourite home infusions is to infuse a citrus forward contemporary gin (see page 61) with good-quality Earl Grey tea. Simply steep the Earl Grey in (ideally loose leaf), and wait. No need to heat, just a gentle stir every so often to let the bergamot oils seep into the spirit while the tea leaves add an underlying tannin to the gin. After half an hour or so (taste and judge), filter the tea out and you'll be left with something highly aromatic and deep in character.

The result is spectacular in a G&T, but even more so in a punch.

We subscribe to the Barbadian punch rhyme as our rule of thumb for how to dose a bowl, working in parts as opposed to exact measures. As the ditty goes, 'One of Sour, Two of Sweet, Three of Strong and Four of Weak'. Barbados might be a rum country, but the measures and principles involved span the spirit genres. For the infusion above, try lemon juice, honey water (½ honey/½ boiling water), Earl Grey-infused gin and soda water (or prosecco if you are feeling naughty!).

We also love taking the most juniper forward gin we can find, for example Southwestern's The Seadog Navy Strength Gin, and adding a mix of nectarine and the skin of two perfectly ripe peaches, as well as a vanilla pod. Leave it to macerate for a day, filter out the botanicals from the gin and add the smallest amount of wildflower honey, sweetening it to taste. Use the home infusion as you would a normal gin, and in a G&T. The likes of lemon thyme, rosemary or lavender as a garnish will accentuate even further. For us, this infusion combination takes us to the South of France in summer; sappy pine trees, the scent of sun cream and the sweet earthiness of the ground that's been scorched by the sun. Evocative, unique and moreish!

Tips for Making Home Infusions

The three key areas to hold in your mind in order to perfect an infusion are sweetness, direct contact (or not) and oxidisation.

It's all too easy to want to add sugar when you add the fruit (many do when they make their sloe gins), but it's advisable, and logical, to wait until you have steeped the fruit in, filtered it out and been able to assess how much it needs first. Add sugar or sweetener at the last possible moment as this will allow you to dose it to perfection.

For sloe and other hedgerow gins, it is important to leave the spirit to penetrate deep into the flesh over an extended period of time (and often helping it on its way by piercing the skin before you steep and giving it a quick stir once in while). Adding the fruit to the gin seems like the only way to go about an infusion, but it is not necessarily the best, especially if heat is involved. To make a rhubarb infusion, it is better to gently heat the fruit with a little water, and then press it to obtain the juice to add to the gin, rather than placing raw stalks in the bottle for a few weeks or actually heating the gin when the stalks are in being steeped.

Opt for a gin with a high ABV, as the infusion process will naturally take some booze out (the fruit soaks it in), and whatever you choose to macerate, keep it somewhere cool as the process is underway to avoid any natural fermentation occuring.

Last, but not least, be mindful of oxidisation. It is better to decant your Fruit Gin into two smaller bottles than it is to have a half empty one. Natural oxidation that occurs in a bottle can turn even the most resplendent of red hues a muddy brown, while the vivid nature of the top notes can dissipate on the aroma. The infused gin won't go 'off' per se, but it will not be as clear as when you first do it.

THE PERFECT GIN & TONIC

After covering how to imbibe almost everything else to this point, it is only appropriate that we sit back and sip such an icon to conclude this condensed guide to all things gin.

It is almost impossible to imagine, let alone find, a more quintessential pairing across any spirit category than gin and tonic. So ubiquitous is the combination that even when you reduce it to three characters, G&T, everyone, will understand what you are talking about. While the concoction may seem simple, both its history and the dizzying array of gin, tonic and garnish combinations make it far from an ordinary drink.

The history of the G&T as we know it starts in the era of the East India Trading Company and British colonial India (from a drinks perspective – from 1780 to 1860). We know that British troops would mix their medicinal quinine with spirit to make it more palatable and it is clear that gin was one of the chosen mixers. (Quinine is first recorded as a treatment for malaria as early as 1631 around the city of Rome, with large scale use of quinine as a prophylaxis starting around 1850.)

The rise of the gin and tonic as a *recreational* drink can be traced back to the early days of Queen Victoria in the 1840s and to the expatriates returning from the colonies where they had developed a taste for the concoction.

For drinks historians, the big debate lies in whether or not a G&T in those days was carbonated, and it is possible that during the era of the British Raj the G&T changed dramatically.

Many claim that carbonated drinks were not that widely available in the nineteenth century, if at all, and the 'tonic' may have been more akin to a syrup. There is some limited evidence of carbonated drinks making their way across the globe, but it is not likely to have been that widespread. The person reported to have developed the first practical process to manufacture bottled carbonated mineral water (based on a process discovered by Englishman Joseph Priestley in 1767) was Johann Jacob Schweppe, but his Indian tonic water, Schweppes, only became popular in the mid-1830s. Regardless of the G&T being a pill, chased down by a dram of gin, a syrupy concoction or a fizzy drink as we know it today – in the space of a century one of the greatest drinks of all time had been invented.

It is amusing that this life-saving invention to make medicine more palatable has today grown into a quest not dissimilar to the hunt for the holy grail: the hunt for the perfect G&T. As you get caught up in inevitable debate on how to make a 'perfect' G&T, keep the gin and tonic origin story in mind, along with some healthy perspective, and remember the two points about context on page 35.

While many will agonise over which gin, tonic and garnish to pick, it is important to remember that the ratio of gin to tonic plays an important part in creating the ultimate serve too. One part gin to three parts tonic is a great place to start, but do not let anyone convince you that it is sacrilegious to change this formula either!

Regionality plays a key factor in preferences over how much to mix in a glass. According to all our data, the Spanish tend to serve a one to four part G-to-T ratio. Contrary to this, in the UK there has been a clear trend since 2014 towards one part gin to only two parts tonic.

To reach a perfect harmony, one must look at the attributes of both gin and tonic independently. Some gins suit boozier ratios, while others need more tonic. It is essential to remember this and not just default into a particular habit.

Flavoured tonics, in particular, offer up some of the biggest challenges when it comes to ratios. While even Indian tonic is not neutral in flavour, the abundance of flavour in some tonics adds both a new dimension and requires some judicious decision making as to what is right. It is all too easy to drown a deliberately subtle, delicate gin and all too easy to undercut a big punchy gin, making it seem much more aggressive. In this dance there are two partners and for an enchanting and enthralling experience, the two have to complement each other.

TONIC

It is with no exaggeration that we say that British brand Fever-Tree was instrumental to the revival of the gin and tonic. Before Fever Tree's launch in 2005, you could choose Schweppes or a supermarket offering (depending on which country you are based in, that is, as, for example, in France this is still not something that is easy to find despite the nation's love affair with sparkling water).

A niche trend started in the American bar scene for 'house tonic', in which cinchona bark is steeped with water and other botanicals and used as a syrup alongside soda, or added to a soda syphon. While it offered an alternative to Schweppes, many forgot just how bitter cinchona (from which you derive quinine) actually is and because of that it was not always pleasant to drink. The idea of an accessible premium alternative to tonic was revolutionary.

We are now in a new era for tonic, and other mixers, with greater focus on using natural ingredients and perfecting the flavour partnership and how each tonic water pairs with gin.

Fever-Tree has remained at the head of the charge with a large portfolio of flavours including Elderflower, Mediterranean and Lemon Tonic. Meanwhile, German-based Thomas Henry Tonic Water has enjoyed huge success with its range, and Spanish made 1724 Tonic Water has been fizzing in glasses across Europe with increasing regularity since 2016. They are all excellent.

For those in Australia, some of the best brands of tonic to look into are Capi, StrangeLove and Daylesford and Hepburn. All three combine a range of flavours, from natural Indian tonic to more peculiar native botanical-infused flavoured varieties. The effervescence in Capi is something to behold in particular!

Often forgotten about and enjoying a new lease of life is British made Fentimans, whose flavoured tonics and bold use of natural colour are worthy of turning heads and filling glasses, while their more classic Connoisseurs Tonic Water pairs well across many gins on the market today.

Schweppes are still the market leaders globally, and with their centuries-long heritage they enjoy the rightfully earned status as the original tonic brand. With increasing unease about the use of HFCS and aspartame, Schweppes also have a 'premium' range that uses natural sugar sources – a move that has seen many revisit the brand.

It's now relatively easy to get hold of tonic syrups too – harking back to the original G&T experience.

London-based small-batch makers BTW have created a balanced recipe that suits classic and contemporary gins alike, while Tennessee makers Jack Rudy have a delicious tonic syrup with a fresh grapefruit zing. When using them, add a splash in the glass (around 10 ml/2 teaspoons) alongside the gin, and top with soda water.

GARNISHES

One of the main causes for people thinking they dislike G&Ts is poor-quality tonics, along with warm mixers and/or wrong ratios. Once you've chosen your preferred ratio and picked the right tonic, your attention must turn to garnishing.

Gin can work with many different garnishes and the variances are more about what inherent flavours you are looking to enhance in the gin, rather than whether something is right or wrong.

The typical go to for most is lime, which in itself is no bad thing. For many gins, especially those with juniper forward profiles (classic gins), this is the perfect choice as the sharp citrus can cut back some of the punchier gins into a mélange of bright flavours. If you are really stuck and don't know what to expect the gin to taste like, a safer all round citrus to lean towards is lemon, which we'd recommend as noting down as your fail safe. It may not have the zing of lime, nor the fleshy warmth of orange, but it'll pair up well with a majority of contemporary gins if you had to pick just the one option ahead of knowing what gin you were serving. However, there is a world of variations to explore and a particular choice of garnish can take a G&T in a completely new flavour direction. Moreover, picking one garnish over another is the easiest thing to do

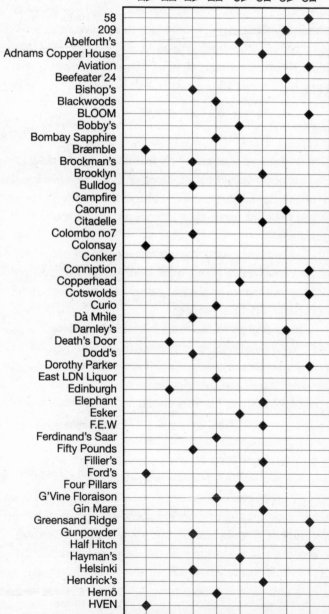

	Lime Wedge	Lime Peel	Lemon Wedge	Lemon Peel	Orange Wedge	Orange Peel	Grapefruit Wedge	Grapefruit Peel
Isle of Harris				◆				
Isle of Wight			◆					
Jawbox							◆	
Jensen's			◆					
Jinzu		◆						
Ki No Bi						◆		
Kirkjuvagr					◆			
Koval				◆				
Lakes						◆		
Makar			◆					
Malfy		◆						
Martin Miller's			◆					
Masons	◆							
McHenry						◆		
McQueen	◆							
Monkey 47								◆
Napue			◆					
Nginious!						◆		
No.3							◆	
Old Bakery				◆				
Opihr					◆			
Persie (Citrus)			◆					
Pickering's	◆							
Pink Pepper								◆
Pinkster				◆				
Plymouth								◆
Poetic License							◆	
Porter's		◆						
Portobello Road							◆	
Pothecary								◆
Renegade								◆
Rock Rose			◆					
Rutte Celery						◆		
Sacred							◆	
Scapegrace					◆			
Shortcross								◆
Silent Pool		◆						
Sipsmith	◆							
Sir Robin of Locksley								◆
Slingsby			◆					
St George Terroir					◆			
Strathearn							◆	
Tanqueray No.TEN								◆
Tarquin's				◆				
The Botanist		◆						
TOAD	◆							
Two Birds							◆	
Victory								◆
Warner Edwards Rhubarb						◆		
William Chase			◆					

in order to alter any gin towards your personal taste preferences.

The following are rules of thumb that tend to work. The trick to success is asking yourself which is the signature 'note' that you recognise when tasting the gin neat. Once you have that in mind, ask yourself if you want to accentuate it (more of the same), complement it (by adding something supportive of it) or contrast it.

With a spiced gin, try an orange wheel as this warming and soft fruit complements botanicals such as clove, nutmeg, cinnamon and cassia. To contrast a spiced gin, lime is often a good choice as its caustic zing can help refresh the profile.

For a citrussy gin, consider balancing it out with flat-leaf coriander or basil, which can add a little punch to the lemon while providing leafy depth. Alternatively, star anise can add a touch of wonderfully exotic contrast, especially to lively citrus botanicals like lime, lemon or grapefruit peel.

For floral gins, a grapefruit peel can add just a touch of freshness without upsetting the delicate aromas. So too can a thin slice of apple. To accentuate the flavours and create a heady aromatic mix in floral gins, a sprig of rosemary can be a perfect complement to lavender forward gins.

Vice versa, a lavender stem not only looks beautiful, it adds a touch of fresh meadows to herbal-lead gins. Furthermore, a wedge of apple in the place of lemon or lime can help provide a touch of acidity without adding citrus and really complements herbaceous gins.

GLASS SHAPE

The highball remains the most popular choice of glass for a G&T in the UK, both in terms of the amount of bars who serve their G&Ts in it, as well as in all of the surveys we have undertaken.

Long peels look at their most appetising when served in a highball, so if that sounds like you, this is the glass for you. Also, for those who love cucumber (perhaps with Hendrick's Gin), they provide the opportunity to show off your skills in a spectacular display, wrapping a thin cucumber slice (also known as a tongue) around the inside.

The copa glass was first popularised in Spain and has since become a staple of G&T culture globally. This vessel suits more adventurous garnishes as it holds the aroma bouquet perfectly, so if you are into 'dual garnishing', this is one for you! Try combinations like an orange wedge and cardamom pods to see for yourself.

Often overlooked, the rocks glass is a perfect vessel for G&Ts as the shorter glass and typically wider diameter (compared to the highball) means that garnishes tend to be closer to the nose, thus giving more aroma impact to the drinker. As they tend to be able to contain less liquid, they are also ideal vessels for boozier ratios of G-to-T.

We would recommend rocks glasses for those who think they might enjoy mint sprigs, basil leaves or citrus wheels (as opposed to a wedge or a peel) as a garnish, or who use larger ice cubes (which take longer to melt, staying colder for longer).

Highball

Copa

Rocks

THE LAST SIP

And so concludes our one-stop shop for all things gin —
we hope you have found this book useful. The category has
enjoyed many changes since the turn of the millennium, but
none more so than the uptake in advocacy and enthusiasm
for the spirit by you, the discerning drinker. We thank
you for this and so, too, do distillers and barkeeps all over
the world.

   We intended this book to be a deliberately quick read
to take you from fumbling around in the supermarket
aisles to ordering like a pro. If you want to dive deeper
into the category, here are some must-read resources to
continue your journey.

For history
Both *Craze: Gin and Debauchery in an Age of Reason* by
Jessica Warner and *The Dedalus Book of Gin* by Richard
Barnett cover the history of gin in great detail, whilst also
managing the arduous task of making it relatable, well-
researched and entertaining.

For more detail
The Curious Bartender's Gin Palace by Tristan Stephenson
and Difford's Guide *Gin: The Bartender's Bible* are not only
great resources covering some history, cocktails and brands,
they also look beautiful and are rich with imagery.

For G&T lovers

While we are inevitably biased, we'll simply say that *A little book on gins, tonics & garnishes* by Gin Foundry has more pairing suggestions, tasting notes and advice than any other out there when it comes to how best to making a cracking gin and tonic.

GinFoundry.com

Find us and our weekly articles of insight, interviews, news, reviews and tips (there are over 300 distillers covered already, featuring some 900 + gins) here.

ACKNOWLEDGEMENTS

To fully acknowledge all of the people who have helped make this book possible would require a manuscript in itself. Just like the story of gin, there have been years of learning and hundreds of people involved.

The learning curve continues each day, and we would like to thank all who have given their time and their knowledge to answer our questions, teach us about how they make their gins, share with us their ideas in such impassioned ways and help build our understanding of what gin is all about.

Patient distillers, historians, bartenders, brand ambassadors, drinks statisticians and fellow writers – we are deeply grateful for you accepting us in your community and for every thing you have helped with on our voyage of discovery here at Gin Foundry. To all the friends and family who have supported us, donned a pinny at our events, packed vans and pushed us through the long nights, we are indebted to you. Leah, Freddy and Rajiv – thank you for having been part of our team.

One person above all needs to be mentioned and thanked in particular. Julia – none of this would be possible without your continued support as we follow our dream. More importantly, none of this journey would have even started without your encouragement. To steal your words and add to them – curiosity unlocks creativity, but it's self-belief (or in this case, yours projected onto to us) that allows for the confidence to pursue it.

INDEX